KU-201-067

Contents

'. . . children are especially vulnerable.
They have not formed the defences
inside themselves which older people have,
and, therefore, need especial protection.
They are also a country's most valuable
asset for the future.'

Mr Justice Latey, Re X [1975] Fam 47 at 52

Editor

Allan Levy QC is the author of three books on child law and contributor of legal notes to Child Abuse Review. He has provided the contribution on the Cleveland Inquiry.

Contributors

Margaret Adcock is a social work consultant and guardian ad litem.

Graham Anthony is a detective sergeant in the South Wales Constabulary.

Margery Bray is a social work consultant.

John Ellison is a solicitor in private practice.

Seán Enright is a barrister.

Michael Hinchliffe is a solicitor in the Official Solicitor's department.

Jane Jenkins is the child abuse co-ordinator for the South Glamorgan Social Services.

Anthony Kilkerr is a detective chief superintendent in the Metropolitan Police.

The Hon Mr Justice Waterhouse is a High Court judge.

Dr Jane Watkeys is a consultant community paediatrician, South Glamorgan Health Authority.

Dr Stephen Wolkind is a consultant child psychiatrist, Maudsley Hospital.

Dr Jane Wynne is a consultant paediatrician, Leeds General Infirmary.

Introduction

Allan Lovy QC

The idea for this book – focusing on child abuse by way of a number of expert contributions from various perspectives – stemmed from a very successful Hawksmere seminar on the subject held in February 1988 under the chairmanship of a High Court judge, Mr Justice Waterhouse.

Material presented on that occasion has been up-dated and expanded in the light of recent developments. Additional contributions have been obtained.

It is hoped that a wide readership will benefit from this publication which is aimed at everyone concerned about child abuse – whether a specialist or a general reader.

The importance of the subject is self-evident. Recently published statistics from 100 out of 108 local authorities in England reveal that almost 40,000 children are registered as being at risk of child abuse. Figures regarding abused children put out periodically by the NSPCC (see Ch 2) amply demonstrate the dimensions of the problem.

The field is rife with uncertainties and controversies. The Cleveland Inquiry (see Ch 4), for instance, highlighted controversial medical areas in child sexual abuse. The law's uncertainties and fragmentation results in many problems. The Children Bill, going through Parliament at the time of writing, is not likely to be implemented until late 1990 or early 1991 and may then, like most major new legislation, bring uncertainties of its own. Intervention by the social worker or the lack of it gives rise to much debate (see Ch 3). There are no easy solutions and a great deal of material needs to be studied, reflected upon and discussed. The following ten chapters are a contribution.

CHAPTER 1

Allegations of Child Abuse – the Court's Approach

THE HON MR JUSTICE WATERHOUSE

Introduction

The title of this chapter is, in a sense, misleading because no uniform approach has yet been evolved by the courts as a whole. Recent publicised cases, however, notably those arising in Cleveland, have underlined the need for a multi-discipline approach to child abuse and it is timely to outline such guidelines as have emerged from the courts so far.

One of the difficulties is that child abuse is the concern of three quite different types of court. The volume of criminal prosecutions for various types of child abuse is increasing daily and alarmingly, but sentencing is not within the scope of this essay. Although many of you may have strong views as to whether or not a prosecution is appropriate and desirable in a particular case, the decision rests with the Crown Prosecution Service; in general, civil courts and social services departments have no more influence in the matter than any conscientious parent would have (see Re K (Minors) (Wardship: Criminal Proceedings) [1987] 3 WLR 1233). The level of sentencing depends very much on the particular circumstances of each case, not least upon the backgrounds of the defendants, and the guidelines given by the Court of Appeal, Criminal Division, from time to time are necessarily in wide terms. It is sufficient to say that, in recent times, there has been an upward trend in sentencing. Child abuse is a scourge of which there is increasing evidence and individual mitigating factors have to be considered against that daunting background.

More pertinently, as far as this chapter is concerned, the two categories of civil court responsible for decision-making in child abuse cases exercise widely different jurisdictions under the present law. In the Juvenile Court the local authority or any other authorised person has to establish one of the criteria set out in section 1 (2) of the Children and Young Persons Act 1969 and that the child or young person is in need of care or control which he is unlikely to receive unless a care order is made. These criteria present many practical difficulties, although sub-section (a) refers to ill-treatment and sub-section (c) to exposure to moral danger a further difficulty is that, rightly or wrongly, many legal practitioners and social workers regard the decisions of some juvenile courts as, at best, unpredictable and, at worst, contrary to the weight of the evidence.

The High Court, that is, the Family Division Judges sitting in Wardship, exercises a much wider jurisdiction in which the first and paramount consideration is the best interests of the ward of court. Despite the fact that in wardship the court retains a close control over decisions in relation to the child, even when a full care order is made, there has been a very steep rise in recent years in the number of wardship applications by local authorities and this trend continues. Thus, in 1985 there were 2815 originating summonses in wardship and authorities were the plaintiffs in 36% of these, whereas in 1986 there were 3339 originating summonses (a rise of 21%) in which 54% of the plaintiffs were local authorities. These figures may be compared with 622 originating summonses in 1971, in only 2.5% of which were local authorities involved. You will readily understand, therefore, that the work of Family Division judges has changed radically and that most of their time is now devoted to wardship cases, many involving allegations of child abuse of one kind or another.

The future of the wardship jurisdiction is uncertain because the Law Commission is engaged in a wide-ranging review of Child Law. Last year it published Working Paper No. 101 on Wards of Court putting forward a number of options and the response to these is not yet known. More importantly for present purposes, the recent Government White Paper on The Law on Child Care and Family Services presented to Parliament in January 1987 proposes that the grounds for the making of a care order in all the relevant jurisdictions other than wardship should be re-cast and assimilated. Three elements will then have to be satisfied for a care order to be made, namely

(a) evidence of harm or likely harm to the child,

(b) that this is attributable to the absence of a reasonable standard of parental care or the child being beyond parental control; and

(c) that the order proposed is the most effective means available to the court of safeguarding the child's welfare.

In this context it is worth quoting para 60 of the White Paper, which reads as follows:

> The three tests will each need to be satisfied. It is intended that 'likely harm' should cover all cases of unacceptable risk in which it may be necessary to balance the chance of the harm occurring against the magnitude of that harm if it does occur. However the test is worded, the court will have to judge whether there is a risk and what the nature of the risk is. The court will also have to make a decision as to whether the harm was caused or will in future be caused by the child not receiving a reasonable standard of care or by the absence of adequate parental control. This is not intended to imply a judgement on the parent who may be doing his best but is still unable to provide a reasonable standard of care. The intention behind the third limb of the grounds—that the order contemplated is the most effective means available to the court of safeguarding the child's welfare—is to direct the court's mind to all the options (including making a supervision order, no order at all or, where it has power, a custody order) in deciding what will be in the child's best interest, or whether the situation will be satisfactorily handled without compulsory measures. It will be essential for the local authority to give the court an idea of their general plans for the child. The amount of detail in the plan will vary from case to case depending on how far it is possible for the local authority to foresee what will be best for the child at the time. There is no intention however to involve the juvenile courts themselves in deciding how the child is to be treated if and when he enters the care of the local authority.

Other important changes are proposed in the White Paper, notably in the grounds for making emergency protection orders (replacing place of safety orders), interim care orders and for discharging care orders but I do not propose to take up space analysing these.

The purpose of referring to them is merely to emphasise that the attention of all courts in care proceedings is likely to be better focused in future on the best interests of the child A more uniform approach will, therefore, be achieved, even though it will still only be in wardship proceedings (if they survive) that the court will retain control over major decisions affecting the child after a full care order has been made.

For these reasons no useful purpose would be served if I were to give an account of the practical difficulties caused by some of the present legal procedures, although they form part of the Cleveland Inquiry report. It will be more relevant and helpful if I adopt the optimistic premise that in future care proceedings in any court the first and paramount consideration should and will be the best interests of the child.

The standard of proof

The general rule in civil proceedings in this country is that he who alleges must prove and that he must establish on a balance of probabilities that the allegation is true. This is, of course, a significantly lower standard than the proof beyond reasonable doubt required in criminal proceedings. It is this general civil standard that is applied at present by juvenile courts in relation to each of the requirements for the making of a care order under section 1 (2) of the Children and Young Persons Act 1969. However, in wardship proceedings, because of the emphasis on the best interests of the child, a different approach is adopted and this may be of critical importance in child abuse cases.

The importance of this point is illustrated by the facts of a recently reported case before Sheldon J, *Re G (a Minor)* [1987] 1 WLR 1461. In that case a child's mother and the grandmother alleged that the child had been sexually abused by the father; and an interim care order, following a place of safety order, had been made by a juvenile court. The local authority subsequently began wardship proceedings and the father applied in these proceedings for care and control

of the child. Having considered the evidence in detail, Sheldon
J said:

> I should at once make it plain that there is no evidence which would
> justify the prosecution of Mr G for any form of sexual abuse or
> improper behaviour with his daughter : the available evidence falls
> far short of the standard of proof beyond reasonable doubt that
> would be needed to lead to a conviction in criminal proceedings,
> as those would be.

In the present context, however, this is not an end of the matter.
In wardship proceedings, as these proceedings are, although alleged
wrongdoing by an individual may be in issue, the predominant
consideration is the welfare of the child and not the behaviour of
any particular adult. They are also civil proceedings.

I agree therefore with Waite J in *In re W (Child Abuse: Evidence)*
[1987] 1 FLR 297, (as indeed I have been invited to by Mrs
Matthews appearing on behalf of Mr G) that in general terms the
standard of proof to be applied in such proceedings as these, is that
based on the balance of probabilities. On the other hand, having
regard to the diversity of issues that might be raised in such
proceedings, I also take the view, as was expressed by Denning LJ
in *Bater v Bater* (1951) P 35, that the 'degree of probability' required
in any particular context may vary and must be 'commensurate with
the occasion' or 'proportionate to the subject matter'. Thus in my
opinion, in such proceedings as the present, a higher degree of
probability is required to satisfy the court that the father has been
guilty of some sexual misconduct with his daughter than would be
needed to justify the conclusion that the child has been the victim
of some such behaviour of whatever nature and whoever may have
been its perpetrator.

In the latter context, indeed, I am of the opinion that the gravity
of the matter is such from the child's point of view that any tilt
in the balance suggesting that she has been the victim of sexual abuse
would justify a finding to that effect. In my view, indeed, there may
also be circumstances in which the application of a 'standard of
proof' as that phrase is commonly understood, is inapt to describe
the method by which the court should approach the particular
problem; as, for example, where the suspicion of sexual abuse or

other wrong-doing, although incapable of formal proof, is such as to lead to the conclusion that it would be an unacceptable risk to the child's welfare to leave him in his previous environment, or (more likely in the case of older children) where, although the court may be satisfied that no sexual abuse has taken place, the very fact that it has been alleged by a child against a parent suggests that in the child's interests, some change in, or control over the existing regime is required.

So also, as has been suggested in the present case, if the child has been the subject of sexual abuse, even if the father cannot be identified as the offender, his character and behaviour, taken in conjunction with all the other circumstances, may lead to the conclusion that it would be an unacceptable risk to her welfare to return her to his care.

In that case Sheldon J went on to consider further evidence and concluded:

> In all the circumstances, however, even applying a more stringent test than a mere 'balance of probabilities', I have been driven to the conclusion, without considering it necessary to spell it out in greater detail, that Mr G has been guilty of an over-familiar and sexually inappropriate relationship with her, amounting in the present context to sexual abuse, which could bode ill for the future and which has created the 'particularly vulnerable' little girl described by Dr Gaye. Nor, in my judgement, is there any evidence to justify the conclusion that anyone but Mr G could be held responsible for that state of affairs.

Accordingly, a care order was made under section 7 (2) of the Family Law Reform Act 1969 on the basis that the child should remain with foster parents with only monthly supervised access by the father.

A rather different description of a similar approach was given by Hollis J in the first major Cleveland test case tried by a High Court judge in July 1987. He was concerned with two families but his decisions were challenged on appeal in relation to only one family and judgment in that appeal, *Re F (Minors)* [1988] 2 FLR 123. It was a case in which Dr Higgs had made diagnoses (supported by Dr Wyatt) of sexual abuse in respect of three daughters aged 9 months to 7 years at the date of the hearing. The judge heard evidence from a large number of experts including Dr Wynne and he made the following important findings:

(1) In the case of each child, the diagnosis of sexual abuse is derived from a clinical examination alone.

(2) In the case of each child, the evidence having been distilled, the diagnosis is of an external penetration of the anus.

(3) None of the children has had a deprived upbringing.

(4) None of the children show any signs of a disturbed child, such as bed-wetting, withdrawal symptoms, overt sexuality or other behavioural problems.

(5) None of the children of school age has been noted at school as behaving other than normally and averagely.

(6) None of the children have complained of having been sexually abused in any way. Those that can speak and understand, indeed, have denied it.

(7) No parent or anyone else has complained of any of the children being sexually abused.

(8) The respective parents seem on the face of it to be estimable people. They were caring parents of happy families. There is abundant evidence to support that assertion by the respective parents and I, having seen them all give evidence before me in the witness box, agree with that finding.

(9) The local authority, through Mr Stewart, do not point an accusing finger at any particular individual as suspected of interfering sexually with any of these children.

(10) Lastly, all the children appear to have led entirely normal and protected lives, and all who can express their feelings wish to go home.

Hollis J went on to consider the proper approach by the wardship court to the evidence in the case and referred to the judgment of Sheldon J quoted above. He commented:

The facts of that case were entirely different to the cases before me, and it must be remembered that judgments are to some extent tailored to suit the facts of the case for decision. It seems, therefore,

that if the risk of a child having been sexually abused while in his
or her family environment is a real, reasonable or distinct
possibility, action should be taken, I think that is really consistent
with what Sheldon J is saying in the case that I have quoted. I do
not consider that a probability has to be shown but a real possibility.
In that way, the interests of the child will be safeguarded.

In the Court of Appeal the approach of standard of proof outlined
by Hollis J was expressly approved by Dillon LJ and it seems that
it was approved implicitly by both Purchas LJ and Nourse LJ. The
case provides therefore, a useful guideline. The judge had ordered
that the children should be returned to their parents but that the
wardship should continue in respect of all three of them because
of some concern about the progress of the youngest child and his
view that all three children should be treated alike. However, the
Court of Appeal, by a majority, having the benefit of further up-to-
date medical evidence, decided that there was no sufficient reason
for continuing the wardship in respect of any of the children. The
majority, that is, Purchas and Nourse LJJ, were particularly
influenced by the argument that continuation of the wardship
would prolong tension within the family unnecessarily, contrary
to the best interests of the children.

I have referred to these cases in some detail because they are highly
topical and because they underline the difficulties facing any court
in doing justice to the parties in a child abuse case at the same
time as making protective decisions in the best interests of the
children. Although I have no authority to speak on behalf of other
judges, I respectfully agree that a higher standard of proof is
appropriate when considering whether a finding should be made
against a specific alleged abuser; but, when deciding what order
is to be made in the best interests of a child, the court should
consider a rather different question, namely, whether there is a
real possibility of harm in the existing or proposed enviroment.
If there is such a risk, it has to be balanced against all the other
relevant factors (see a recent application of the principle by the
Court of Appeal in Re P [1987] 2 FLR 467 in which the baby ward

had been born into a household in which older children had been seriously abused).

The diagnostic process

What I have written so far has been relatively uncontroversial in the sense that it represents the law as it is necessarily administered by the courts under present legislation and procedural rules, difficult though the decisions may be in individual cases. When one turns to the evaluation of evidence, however, one enters a much more difficult and potentially controversial area of discussion. I am conscious also that there may well be a division of opinion at present between judges on the one hand and psychiatrists and social workers on the other.

What seems to me to be a central problem is the assessment of developing procedures for the questioning of children who have complained of sexual abuse or whose behaviour gives rise to the suspicion that they may have been the victims of such abuse. Part of the problem relates to the mode of presentation of such evidence, whether to a criminal court or to a civil court, and the readily understandable wish of doctors and social workers to put before the court the earliest possible evidence of what a child has said and how he or she has said it. There is fierce argument about these matters but I do not propose to deal with that controversy here. What I must discuss is the evaluation of such evidence by the wardship court on the assumption that a videotape and/or transcript of what the child has said is admitted in evidence.

Many of us are familiar now with the work undertaken in the past 5 years or so in the child sexual abuse clinic at Great Ormond Street Hospital for Sick Children by Dr Arnon Bentovim, which has been followed up more recently in some other parts of the country. I can do no better than repeat the summary description of the technique and purpose of the interviews given by the authors of a recent article in the journal *Family Law* (1987, p 151 and see also p 28):

The child is interviewed by a psychiatric social worker and sometimes a doctor. During the course of the interview, use is made of anatomically correct dolls to encourage the child to demonstrate behaviour which she is reluctant or unable to describe in words. Since children are often very reluctant to talk about the matters in issue, the interviewer applies a degree of coaxing and pressure on the child to overcome this reticence. This encouragement to answer may involve leading or hypothetical questions or questions designed to elicit a different answer to one already given. It is felt by the clinic that such pressure is necessary to enable the child finally to make statements against another family member; as one of the clinic staff has put it, it is necessary to match the trauma which the child has suffered through the abuse by placing equal pressure on the child to talk about what has occurred. A transcript of the interview will be taken, and it will also be video-recorded. The interviews originally followed a pre-determined structure, but in the light of criticism from the courts, the structure is now more flexible. Nonetheless, the interviewer starts from the position of wanting to believe the child, not doubting the child's statements.

This type of interview was originally developed to deal with cases where there is already firm evidence of abuse, so that it functioned as a form of therapy to enable the child to recover from the ordeal. These are, in fact, the majority of the cases handled by the clinic. It is comparatively recently that the interview has been used to try to diagnose sexual abuse. Of approximately 500 cases referred to the team, only 100–150 have fallen into the latter category. Thus, while the clinic asserts that in about 95% of cases it finds abuse to have occurred, generally this will be where other evidence supports that finding, and it is not apparent in what proportion of the 'diagnostic' cases abuse is established.

From the courts' point of view these interviews present many difficulties and the problems have been fully discussed in six cases heard in the Family Division in 1986 and reported in the Family Law Reports in 1987 (see [1987] 1 FLR 269 (Ewbank J) 280 (Swinton Thomas J) 293 (Latey J) 297 (Waite J) 310 (Ewbank J) and 321 (Hollis J)). One of the problems already mentioned is that the purpose of such interviews is usually therapeutic; what may be useful for therapy purposes may not, however, be persuasive as evidence of the true facts. Again, most doctors and social workers accept the current conventional wisdom (I do not use the expression critically) that young children are usually truthful when they complain of sexual abuse (their veracity is put as high as 90%) whereas lawyers are inevitably dubious about answers that are prompted by leading questions and, sometimes, sustained pressure. Yet again, the greater the distance in time from the incidents referred to, the staler the complaint will be and lawyers, as a result of their training, view critically complaints that are not 'fresh' and which may have been the subject of previous discussion with the complainant. I will content myself with one quotation from Wait J to underline these concerns. He said in *Re W* at [1987] 1 FLR 303D:

> First, the use of a leading question. The notion of ejaculation was introduced to the child's mind by the question (speaking of penile contact earlier mentioned by the child) 'When daddy does that, does it ever feel a bit wet down there?' The hypothetical type of questioning is illustrated by part of the area of inquiry directed to vaginal stimulus 'What would you say if dad tickles you there and and you didn't like it?' I would say 'Stop it, daddy.' 'Would he stop or carry on?' 'He would carry on'. 'Would he always tickle you in the outside or would he sometimes tickle you a bit in the inside?' 'In the inside'. Cross-examination is exemplified by the following exchange: 'Is there a private bit of dad he would put there?' 'No'. 'Would he put his willy there?' 'No'. 'Does he sometimes put his willy there?' Nods head.

It is not surprising in the light of what I have said that in one of the 6 cases the judge commented that no evidential weight was to be attached to the diagnostic interview and that in *Re W* Waite J said that its assistance was limited to enabling the court to catch the flavour of the interview etc. The problem is an acute one and each case, in particular each interview, has to be assessed on its own merit in the light of the other evidence available. Attention is being paid to judicial criticism and it may be that progressively the evidential value of diagnostic interviews will increase as techniques of interviewing are modified. The most helpful and constructive comment was made by Latey J in the recent case of *Re M* at p 295C and it is worth quoting his comment in full:

> Speaking, I stress, in the most general terms, there seems to me to be two broad categories of child abuse cases coming to the clinic.
>
> First, cases where, from the already existing external evidence, sexual abuse is already established: cases, for example, where there has already been a conviction or an admission or physical medical evidence. Here the clinician can concentrate on the therapy without at the same time considering the forensic aspect. These, on the evidence, are the majority of cases which come to the clinic.
>
> Secondly, cases, such as the instant one, where there is nothing more than a combination ('constellation' it is called) of alerting symptoms. On the evidence, they are a minority. But they are the cases which may well come to the court for decision. How can the clinic best handle them so as to help the court and at the same time perform what, in my view, remains their more important function, the therapeutic one?
>
> The resources of the clinic are not limitless, far from it. Within their limits, what can they do?
>
> What follows is given tentatively and in the belief that it is already in the minds of Dr Bentovim and others. Perhaps, nonetheless, it may be of some help as coming from someone outside the immediate clinical arena.
>
> First, there might be an appraisal at the start of each referral whether the case is likely to fall within the second category. If it does, then secondly, there should always be a video recording. The reason is this: where there is a dispute whether there has or has not been abuse, the court is anxious whether it should accept the ipse dixit of the interviewer or interviewers, however skilled and experienced. This is because cases have shown (two of them have been referred to during the hearing, and there have been others in my experience) that the precise questions, the oral answers (if there are any), the gestures and body movements, the vocal inflexion and

intonation, may all play an important part in interpretation. Where there is a dispute, there should be an opportunity for another expert in the field·to form a view. Often, no doubt, he would reach the same interpretation and conclusion. In other cases he might not, and in the interests not only of justice between the parties but of doing its best to arrive at the truth of the matter in the interests of the child, the court should have the benefit of such evidence, so informed.

Thirdly, and this is much more controversial and even more tentative : in the second category, should there be some difference in the interviewing and questioning technique? In the first category the forensic evidential element seldom, if ever, enters into the matter. The questioners can deal with it with the sole purpose of therapy—to get the child to unburden itself. In the second category, there are, or may be, the two elements, therapeutic and forensic. I simply am not equipped to suggest whether a modification of the technique could be made so as better to meet the forensic need without seriously undermining the therapeutic need. It may not be possible. Or it may be possible. As I see it, it is for the clinical experts to explore this and, perhaps, experiment. I was much impressed by what Dr McClelland had to say or suggest about the approach where there is an initial, tentative diagnosis of abuse. He suggested that in such cases the interview and questioning should be directed in large part toward disconfirming, as he put it, the initial diagnosis. Because, he suggests, if that is done and, nonetheless, at the end of it the diagnosis is abuse, it is a more valid one. To my mind that has much force. At least, it would be helpful to the court if the questioners were alert to any indications of an innocent, as well as a sinister, interpretation and recorded them in their notes, reports and evidence.

Finally—and I think this is repetition—I do want to stress these points : this is a relatively new technique pioneered in this country by Dr Bentovim and his clinic. It has already done truly valuable work. It is still being developed and refined. I have the impression that the suggestions I have tentatively made are already in their minds, but perhaps made from outside they may help to crystallize them from the forensic aspects. But in the end, clinically and therapeutically, they are the experts. All that the lawyers, the judges, can do is to give such help as they can in pointing to the forensic needs. Whether those needs can be met, or entirely met, and met without a serious erosion of the therapeutic needs, is another matter. A balance may have to be struck and that balance may have to be varied as time goes on, and the technique is refined.

Remedial measures and rehabilitation

Throughout the 10 years during which I have sat as a Family Division judge I have been conscious of the limits of the information available to the courts when deciding what orders should be made in children cases generally. The arguments in favour and against proposed courses of action are well rehearsed before us but the back up of research and statistical analysis is sadly limited. Moreover, it is not practicable to reserve individual cases to particular judges indefinitely so that we have all too little information about the ultimate results of the decisions that we make. A further difficulty is that in wardship proceedings the procedure is inevitably adversial when there is a real dispute between the local authority and other parties and it is only in a small percentage of cases that it is justifiable to join the children as parties and to invite the Official Solicitor to act on their behalf. Thus, there were only 385 references to the Official Solicitor in 1985 and the total extant that year was 1415; and even this volume of work imposes a great strain upon the Official Solicitor's limited resources. Similarly, in care proceedings in the Juvenile Court, there are severe practical constraints upon the use of guardians 'ad litem' (see *R v Plymouth Juvenile Court ex parte F & F* [1987] 1 FLR 169). It follows that very frequently the court does not have before it any independent expert assessment of the possible courses of action and the likely results.

In making these comments I must not be thought to be criticising either the competence or the independence of Directors of Social Services and their staffs who, despite often depleted resources, do their work with great professional skill and integrity. Judges do find, however, that the independent view of the Official Solicitor, frequently reinforced by the evidence of a paediatrician or child psychiatrist, is of great assistance in trying to reach a correct decision. There is the added advantage in cases in which a child is sufficiently mature to speak for himself or herself that his or her views can be presented to the court through a responsible filter.

This seems to me to be of special importance in child abuse cases generally. It is notorious that children who complain of sexual abuse by a parent are frequently plagued by feelings of guilt themselves, not least because of the break up of their home that may ensue, and the surviving bond between child and parents is something to which the court must give proper weight if the damage to the child is to be minimised. I believe that the child's voice about his or her future should be heard by the court directly or indirectly whenever that is practicable.

My present impression, and it is no more than that, is that we are still in our infancy in decision-making about remedial measures in child sexual abuse cases. It is well known that such abuse is often repetitive, involving more than one child of the family, and most of us recognise, on a broad public basis, the need for severe deterrent measures under the criminal law in bad cases. The term 'sexual abuse', however, covers a wide spectrum of behaviour and, rightly or wrongly, I think that there may be a danger of hysteria about it in some quarters. My own view is that, if it is at all practicable and home conditions are otherwise adequate, rehabilitation of the child with the family should always be an objective in cases of abuse of a less evil kind. Having said that, however, many of us have been faced with the intractable, and perhaps, insuperable problem of the father who denies any form of abuse, despite strong evidence to establish it, and who is wrongheadedly supported in his denial by the mother.

I have read with great interest accounts of the research by Dr Bentovim and his colleagues into the prognosis for rehabilitation after abuse (published recently in *Adoption and Fostering* (1988) Volume 2) and of similar earlier research by Ruth and Henry Kempe. There is no succinct way in which the court's approach can be summarised because the variety of cases and combinations of circumstances is almost infinite. I believe that the broad principles emerging from recent research are likely to be acted upon by the courts. In particular, the courts may well accept in most cases of serious abuse that acknowledgment of responsibility by the parent involved, and possibly by both parents, is a necessary pre-condition of successful rehabilitation. Even so, however, much may depend upon the nature and gravity of the abuse, the reasons underlying the parents' attitudes and the ages of the children whose future is in question.

Conclusion

I fear that some readers of this chapter may be disappointed that I have not been either more challenging or more decisive in outlining the approach of the court to child abuse. However, I write as one only of many judges who deal with these matters and I have sought to express as general a view as possible. It must be remembered also that each case has to be decided upon the particular evidence before the court. The judge who carries around with him a tool kit of preconceived ideas may not do justice in the individual case before him and is certainly not adopting the correct judicial approach. We hope that with experience we are better equipped to exercise our wide discretion more correctly in the best interests of the children with whom we have to deal but we are not professional doctors, psychologists or social workers; and we must even be wary of carrying from one case to another expert opinions that may not be applicable to different facts and which new parties are unable to test by cross-examination. Our duty is to evaluate the evidence before us and the greater the exchange of views between those involved in child care the greater is the hope that correct, or at least the best, solutions will be found.

CHAPTER 2

Medical Aspects of Child Abuse

DR JANE WYNNE
Consultant paediatrician

Child abuse is only widely recognised within a society where child mortality and morbidity is low and children are expected to live until adult life. At this stage the quality of the child's life may be considered and a child is recognised increasingly as an individual in his own right. In the UK children's rights are discussed but children do not enjoy as privileged a position as many children's professionals would wish, and many adults have difficulty in accepting that the child's interests may conflict with those of their parents. These points are important when considering the types of child abuse which are increasingly recognised in the UK, especially emotional and sexual abuse.

We have learned much about child abuse since our colleagues first recognised 'battered babies' in the early 1960s but still have much to learn.

The rate of registration of children who are thought to have been abused has doubled according to the NSPCC's figures[1] from 1984–7. Much of the recent escalation has been due to the increased recognition of child sexual abuse, a growth of 21% from 1986–7. Although the NSPCC have recorded a recent fall in the numbers of children physically abused, the number of serious injuries has risen, as have the deaths from abuse. The rate of physical abuse in 1987 was 0.85 per thousand children (0–14 years) and the number of fatal and seriously injured children accounted for 14% of these. The NSPCC estimate that in England and Wales over 8000 children aged 0–14 years were physically abused in 1987 and over 7000 children were sexually abused.

The figures we have in Leeds are similar to the NSPCC ones, except that we have noted an increase in all forms of abuse. The numbers of physically abused children have shown a steady rise and the injuries have become more severe in terms of fractures, brain damage and death. The diagnosis of probable child sexual abuse has risen from fewer than 10 children per year in the early 1980s to 237 in 1986, although the numbers now appear to be levelling. Neglect, failure to thrive and emotional abuse are all under-recognised and perhaps increasingly so, as health and social workers attempt to cope with the greatly increased referral rate of children who may have been sexually abused. Much of the work and research in the UK has been concerning physical abuse and neglect; research and even basic data collection in child sexual abuse (CSA) is only now beginning.

The medical recognition of abuse must always be in the context of a full medical examination, including investigations such as X-rays, and the findings then reviewed in the light of the social and sometimes police investigation. The *Report of the Inquiry into Child Abuse in Cleveland* made this clear for CSA, but it is equally true in all forms of abuse. In some situations the medical input to the multi-agency assessment is more significant than others but doctors, or indeed any professional, must not work alone in this field. Physical examination is but one part of a much larger 'jigsaw', and all the cases of abuse must be considered as a whole.

Physical abuse

What is new in the field of physical abuse? The most worrying cases remain the very young, and children between 0–1 years are over-represented in the statistics. It is in the youngest children that the important neurological sequelae, for example following shaking, are usually seen. Shaking may cause brain haemorrhages, haemorrhage behind the eye and death. In survivors cerebral palsy (spasticity), visual impairment, epilepsy and learning disorders are found. Children under the age of 12 months are particularly vulnerable but in 1985 in Leeds a 4-year-old boy was shaken to death.

The important practice point for workers who see an infant with even a small bruise is *take it seriously*. Even two 0.5 cm bruises one on each cheek of a 4-month-old baby are important. Why? The baby could not by virtue of his developmental level cause the bruises himself, and as the baby is totally dependent on his carers he is extremely vulnerable. The inference is that the carer has lost his temper and bruised the child. Although many parents say they have felt like shaking a young baby that cries and cries, most do not. To have lost control, even once, when caring for a tiny baby needs an immediate assessment. This does not necessarily mean taking the baby away from his parents—although the baby must be protected, and this is the professional's first responsibility.

However, the baby may have other signs of abuse :

- Are there other bruises, a torn frenulum, burns, scalds, or other odd marks?
- Is the baby thriving? Obtain the baby's weight chart from the Well Baby Clinic to assess the growth rate.
- What is the baby's development like? Is he a bright, attentive child or pale and disinterested?
- What is the child's general care like? Has he crusted cradle cap, chronic nappy rash, spotty pallid skin?
- Has his general health been good? Has he had his immunisations at 3 months? Look at his previous medical history including birth history. What do the Health Visitor and GP say?

When the child is examined, careful documentation of all the injuries is necessary with measurements, and description of the colour of any bruise, in order to estimate the approximate age of the bruises and whether the injuries are likely to have occurred on one or more occasions. (See Table 1 for ageing of bruises)

Table 1.Rough estimate as to age of bruises

< 24 hours	Red or reddish—purple swollen
1–2 days	Purple—swollen
3–5 days	Starting to yellow
5–7 days	Yellow, fading
> 1 week	Yellow, brown, fading

What disorders must the doctor consider when looking at a bruised child? The differential diagnosis includes bleeding and clotting disorders. A blood film and clotting studies will rule out the major conditions such as idiopathic thrombocytopenic purpura or a clotting disorder for example haemophilia.

A skeletal survey will usually be carried out in children aged 2 years or less. This is an X-ray of all the child's bones and because of the irradiation given to the child, should not be done without due consideration and consent with proper explanation to the parents. The reason for the X-rays is to look for previously unrecognised injuries, ie healing fractures.

Recently there has been interest in the possibility of fragile bone disease presenting as non-accidental injury. Copper deficiency in infancy has also been suggested as a cause of multiple fractures in infancy. There have been useful review articles in the medical press on both these disorders.[2-4]

In the commoner forms of fragile bone disease, a child may be born with many fractures; or, in the first few months of life fractures may result in the course of normal handling. There is usually a family history of this disorder. Other members of the family may have a blue tinge to the whites of their eyes (sclerae), be deaf, or have abnormal teeth.

Problems occasionally arise when the question is asked in an infant with severe fractures: is this fragile bone disease? There is a rare Type IV variant which occasionally occurs without a family history of the disorder, the sclerae are not blue and there are no other features of the disease. However, further fractures would occur in foster-care if this were the case.

Dr L S Taitz of Sheffield has estimated that the chance of such a sequence of events would be in the order of 1 case every 100–300 years in Sheffield.[2]

Copper deficiency has been recognised for more than 30 years as a cause of anaemia, skeletal abnormalities and fractures. Rib fractures in copper deficiency have only been recorded in premature babies and skull fractures have never been described. All the children with fractures (a late manifestation of copper deficiency) had obviously abnormal bones. The consensus is that copper deficiency is very unlikely to occur in a healthy term infant fed either breast milk or a standard formula. If the bones are normal apart from the fractures this also excludes a diagnosis of copper deficiency. Predisposing features are prematurity, total parenteral nutrition (feeding by infusion into a blood vessel) or a copper-deficient milk. If these are excluded by the history, and there are no other features of a copper deficiency shown by blood tests and otherwise normal bones, it is very unlikely that fractures are due to copper deficiency. But it is important for a specialist radiologist to review the X-ray films.

Tables 2 and 3 will help to show how these disorders may be differentiated from child abuse.

Table 2. Osteogenesis imperfecta or fragile bone disease

1. Rare, found in 1/20,000 births
2. Family history in 80% of cases
3. Blue sclerae commonly seen
4. Other X-ray abnormalities
5. Other relatives have hypermobile joints, deafness, abnormal teeth
6. Types 2 and 3 are severe and do not cause confusion with NAI

Table 3. Copper deficiency

HISTORY	BLOOD TESTS	BONES
(1) Premature baby	(1) Anaemic	(1) Bones thin
(2) Artificial feeding on copper-deficient feeds	(2) Low copper level in blood	(2) All bones affected
		(3) Not skull fractures
		(4) Rib fractures (only premature babies)

Neglect, failure to thrive and emotional abuse

Neglect, failure to thrive and emotional abuse are all under-recognised. The NSPCC statistics show that registration for failure to thrive represents only 3% of the total of children registered because of abuse. This means roughly 500 children in England and

Wales were registered in this category in 1987. Each health visitor, clinic doctor, GP, and certainly the staff on each paediatric ward will recognise that this is a gross underestimate.

Assessment of children who are failing to thrive includes compiling a growth chart, to check growth rate. A medical examination and sometimes investigations are needed to rule out organic causes for the child's poor weight gain, such as coeliac disease or cystic fibrosis. If the child puts on weight dramatically on admission to hospital this is good additional information. Non-organic failure to thrive accounts for well over half of all referrals to hospital because of failure to thrive.

Part of the assessment is to take a dietary history, and the opinion of a paediatric dietician can be very helpful. Beware however of 'food-lies'! Parents may describe enormous meals, given at frequent intervals, that are enough to feed a baby elephant, yet it may be that the parents feel that the professional should hear this rather than a more accurate description. Asking parents to keep a diary is another way of making an assessment but best of all may be for the Health Visitor to drop in at a meal time and observe what is happening. Emotional problems are often inextricably bound up with feeding difficulties and these should be explored. In other families a lack of organisation, often associated with poverty, leads to a chaotic life style where adequate meals are not available to the child at frequent enough intervals and so the child just does not eat enough calories to grow and put on weight. These children may also have delayed development and signs of emotional disturbance.

A developmental check of children who have been abused is part of the paediatric assessment. In the under-fives, the paediatrician often has the skills to undertake a brief analysis but in older children, or more complex situations, a child psychiatrist or psychologist is able to give a more in depth view of the child's development as well as the emotional aspects. In general, only in the most severe cases of neglect or emotional deprivation will skills such as walking be retarded, but commonly the child will have delayed language development and poor social skills. He will often be quiet, apathetic, lack inquiry or investigation in his play and show little affection, smiling infrequently. He may be clingy and attention seeking with adults yet unable to relate to his own peer group. Other emotionally deprived children may be the converse in that they are over-active, lack concentration, may be aggressive, fighting, biting, scratching, spitting and having spectacular temper tantrums. Older children lie, steal, truant, and drift into other antisocial activities such as glue sniffing.

Neglected children are the opposite of our expectation of childhood, that is, bright, alert, inquiring with a ready smile, affectionate behaviour with a natural reserve, and physically fit with plenty of energy, shining hair, firm muscle, 'glowing' skin.

Neglected and emotionally abused children in general do badly and we do not have the skills or resources to help them adequately; there are many such children in our society. Poverty is a major stress factor and important in child neglect and physical abuse. Emotional abuse is recognised in all social groups; physical abuse is much less common in materially well off homes.

Child sexual abuse

Child sexual abuse has been the most recently recognised and the most hotly debated form of abuse in the UK. Fortunately the *Report of the Inquiry into Child Abuse in Cleveland*[5] was presented in June 1988 and many basic issues have now been clarified. The Judicial Inquiry was chaired by Mrs Justice Butler-Sloss (now a Court of Appeal judge) and assisted by three Assessors, Professor David Hull (Professor of Child Health), Mr John Chant (Director of Social Services), Mr Leonard Soper, (a retired Chief Constable).

The final conclusions of the Report open with the statement:

> We have learned during the Inquiry that sexual abuse occurs in children of all ages, including the very young, to boys as well as

girls, in all classes of society and frequently within the privacy of the family. The sexual abuse can be very serious and on occasions includes vaginal, anal and oral intercourse. The problems of CSA have been recognised to an increasing extent over the past few years by professionals in different disciplines. This presents new and particularly difficult problems for the agencies concerned in child protection.

It is clear that as our colleagues began to recognise the the extent of physical abuse in the 1960s, so we are now recognising CSA in the 1980s. Henry Kempe, an American paediatrician, in 1979 said that society went through various stages in the recognition of abuse.[6]

- Denial that any abuse exists to a significant extent in the community as a whole.
- 'Battered babies' recognised initially, and then less severe forms of physical abuse.
- Physical abuse is better handled and neglect, failure to thrive, and more subtle forms of abuse such as 'poisoning' are recognised.
- Emotional abuse and neglect and a pattern of severe rejection seen.
- The community pays attention to the serious plight of the sexually abused child.
- The community guarantees each child is truly wanted, given loving care, decent shelter, food, first class preventive and curative health care.

By the mid-1980s many areas were somewhere between stages 3 and 4 in the recognition of child abuse.

It was only in 1988, to coincide with the publication of the 'Cleveland Report' that the DHSS finally produced their document *Working Together*[7] and *Diagnosis of Child Sexual Abuse; Guidance for Doctors*.[8]

The delay in producing these helpful documents is, I think, due to the problem society has in accepting sexual abuse occurs and until the 'Cleveland Report' many people felt happier to believe sexual abuse of children was an aberration found only in Leeds or Middlesbrough. Mrs Justice Butler-Sloss commented 'How society acknowledges the existence of, recognises and then handles CSA poses difficult and complex problems'. There are many problems and we are only just at the beginning.

Our work in Leeds shows the problem is a real one—and a bigger one than we envisaged. We (Dr C Hobbs and I) now see over 1000 children each year— half referred because of possible sexual abuse and the rest because of all the other abuses. We diagnose probable sexual abuse in about 250 children each year.

We use the Kempe definition[6] of CSA :

> Sexual abuse is defined as the involvement of dependent, developmentally immature children and adolescents in sexual activities they do not truly comprehend, to which they are unable to give informed consent, or that violate the social taboos of family life.

The average age of the children we see in Leeds is less than 7 years and the average age of the children has fallen each year. Around 40% of children present following an allegation by them of abuse, and the rest because of sexually explicit play or behaviour, medical symptoms such as vaginal bleeding, physical abuse, psychosomatic or behavioural disorder. Although the traditional picture is of a teenage girl abused by her step-father this is an out-dated view. One-third of the children are younger than 5 years old and we see 1.8 girls for every boy. It is necessary to see all the children in a family, as if one child is abused it is usual that other siblings are too, and this includes boys as well as girls. One-third of the children are abused by their natural father, and two-thirds within the close family, which means cohabitee, uncle, grandfather or older brother. The number of teenagers who abuse worries us. Statistics suggest 75% of abusers began abusing in their teenage years and 25% of the Leeds abusers are teenagers. Women may abuse as well : in our data 10–15% of abusers are women, and this is probably an underestimate. Again natural mothers and teenage girls are the two main groups of abusers

Abusers are currently being studied but they clearly come from all social classes. Whilst the fixated paedophile is a menace to children, the other main group of abusers appears to be men who are extremely sexually active and promiscuous and just want sexual activity. In this latter group there is an overlap between those who abuse children, rape, expose themselves, and indecently assault. Sexual abusers may abuse very large numbers of children— a recent American study showed an average of seven children with a range of 1–40 abuses by each abuser. Women have only recently been recognised as abusers and they are an even less well recognised and understood group.

Physical examination whilst an important part of the investigation of CSA has been greatly over-emphasised—mainly by the media. Over half the children in our series have no abnormality on physical examination and it is only in a few instances such as a child of 3 years with gonorrhoea, or a girl with vaginal tears, or a child with anal tears, or where forensic tests confirm the presence of semen that the examination takes on a greater significance than the usual 'compatible with' statement. In any event, the physical examination of the genitalia and anus is part of the whole medical examination, which includes the child's story, the medical history, as well as a complete physical examination looking for bruises and other injuries and a determination of growth, development and emotional state.

If the abuser admits to the abuse that makes the entire exercise so much easier! The medical examination must ultimately be seen in conjunction with the social work and police investigation.

The physical signs associated with CSA are described in *Lancet* papers.[9,10] The signs are of trauma, that is bruising, laceration, stretching or tearing (of the hymen or anus). There may be super-added infection and a differential diagnosis of other medical conditions is considered. Like any trauma, healing takes place and if examination is delayed or repeated after weeks or months there may be return to normality, although in a few cases, scars will be seen.

Of importance in developing a service for sexually abused children is having an understanding by all adults that sexual abuse exists, that we should listen to children and act to protect them from further abuse. The professionals must then develop networks and have access to informed opinion and advice.[5,7] The children and their families will also need access to therapy—as Anna Freud[11] so clearly stated:

> Where the chances of harming a child's normal development are concerned it (ie incest or other forms of CSA by parental figures) ranks higher than abandonment, neglect, physical maltreatment or any other form of abuse. It would be a total mistake to under-rate the implication or frequency of its actual occurrence.

We do not have available to our patients adequate therapy, as we do not have any increase in resources to help with the currently recognised endemic sexual abuse.

We have a local agreement that children are not seen in police stations, and we try to ensure they are seen by suitably trained doctors (usually paediatricians) in a quiet, child-centred environment. The doctors spend time, talk to the children, reassure, answer questions and hope to start to restore some of the child's lost confidence. If the child asks to see a doctor of a particular gender we try to arrange this. Sedation and general anaesthetics are rarely needed. The child's consent, however, is needed, and more formally that of the parents. Facilities are needed for taking bacteriological specimens to look for sexually transmitted disease. Forensic tests will be done if the child is seen shortly after a sexual assault. Pregnancy tests and the 'morning-after-pill' may be prescribed with appropriate counselling.

The hospital or community paediatrician is in a good position to work with social services departments, the police, and also other health professionals such as psychologists and psychiatrists. They are also able to follow up their patients to ensure that healing has occurred, treatment of infection has been adequate and also to review any emotional difficulties the child may be experiencing.

The 'Cleveland Report' is clear on the duties of the examining doctor (who may come from a variety of backgrounds) but who has responsibilities for the child, his medical and forensic investigation, report writing (for social services and the police) as well as attendance at case conferences and court (care or criminal proceedings). The recommendation that each district has a list of suitably trained doctors and a Specialist Assessment Team (social worker, police, doctor) to advise on difficult or complex cases would help standardise investigation and management and also prevent the child being repeatedly examined and interviewed. The use of videos may help in the avoidance of repeated interviews but should only be used by skilled interviewers—as a poor interview and hence video may make it more difficult to protect the child in the courts. It is as well to remember child abuse is what the courts say it is, not the professional workers, and the courts will be asked to assess increasingly complex cases.

Child abuse in all its forms is disruptive, and denies the child his right to an abuse-free childhood. The effect of abuse may be far reaching and affect the child adversely for the rest of his life. The child may die, be brain damaged or have emotional scars which are every bit as disabling as some of the evident neurological deficits seen in our children. A child of 6 years, who is hit too hard, once, by his father at a moment of great stress is not at real risk of emotional damage and is at one end of a spectrum which extends to children who are the victims of neglect, deprivation and depravation about which we hear too frequently. If our society is to think of itself as civilised we should now stand back, disentangle adult or parental rights from children's rights and plan for a future which will allow each child the rights we would wish for our own children.

References

1. Creighton, S J *Child Abuse in 1987—Initial findings from the NSPCC's Register Research* NSPCC Research Briefing No 9 (1988)

2. Leader *Child Abuse and Osteogenesis Imperfecta* British Medical Journal Vol 295 pp 1082–3 (1987)

3. Leader *Copper and the Infant* Lancet pp 900–1 (1987)

4. Leader *Child Abuse or Copper Deficiency. A radiological view* British Medical Journal Vol 294 p 1370 (1987)

5. Butler-Sloss, E *Report of The Inquiry Into Child Abuse in Cleveland 1987* Cm 412, HMSO (1988)

6. Kempe, R I and Kempe, C H *Child Abuse* Fontana/Open Books, London (1978)

7. *Working Together: a guide to arrangements for inter-agency co-operation for the protection of children from abuse* DHSS and The Welsh Office, HMSO (1988)

8. *Diagnosis of Child Sexual Abuse; Guidance for doctors* DHSS HMSO (1988)

9. Hobbs, C J and Wynne, J M *Buggery in Childhood—a common syndrome of child abuse* Lancet 11 pp 792–6 (1986)

10. Hobbs, C J and Wynne, J M *Child Sexual Abuse—an increasing rate of diagnosis* Lancet 11 pp 837–42 (1987)

11. Freud, A *A Psychoanalysts's View of Sexual Abuse by Parents* In P B Mrazek and C H Kempe (eds) *Sexually Abused Children and their Families* Pergamon Press, Oxford (1981)

CHAPTER 3

Issues
for
Social
Workers

MARGARET ADCOCK

Social work consultant

The legal definitions of the social worker's role are apparently quite clear. Local authorities have a duty to provide a child protection service, although as Blom Cooper QC pointed out in 'A Child in Mind' [1] there is no agreed definition of a child protection service. The Children and Young Persons Act 1969 imposes a duty to investigate and bring care proceedings when there appear to be grounds. This implies that social work intervention consists of investigation—followed in some cases by a Place of Safety Order which separates child and family—followed probably by care proceedings and perhaps a period of 2–9 months before a final court decision. Once there is an interim care order or reception in care there is a duty to make the long-term welfare of the child the first consideration (Child Care Act 1980, section 18).

In practice, intervention poses a series of dilemmas for social workers which reflect the ambivalence, ignorance and uncertainty of (a) society at large, (b) other professionals, (c) social workers themselves, about the whole issue of child protection and the nature of their professional role.

Many of the dilemmas were identified in the Report of the Inquiry into Child Abuse in Cleveland[2] and in a paper given by Bentovim[3] at the Seventh International Conference of Child Abuse and Neglect. The dilemmas are:

- how far should the need to protect children be balanced against the need to avoid excessive interference in family life, ie what is the balance between the needs of children and the rights of parents?
- how much autonomy in decision-making do social workers and other professionals have? What happens if the courts and the general public disagree with the goals and methods of treatment prescribed by the professionals?
- what should be the main forms of social service work in child abuse?

The needs of children and the rights of parents

Social workers now may well feel that they will be criticised whatever they do. The Inquiries into the deaths of Jasmine Beckford, Tyra Henry and Kimberley Carlile were all critical of social workers' failure to recognise that children were being severely abused and should have been removed from their parents. In the Cleveland Report, however, social workers were criticised for being over zealous, for removing too many children, and for denying access and information to their parents.

It is clearly difficult to find an appropriate and acceptable middle way between the two extremes criticised in the Report. To do so it seems that social workers have to address three questions:

- is there sufficient evidence to establish a diagnosis of abuse?
- if there is a diagnosis of abuse, how serious are the implications? Is it safe for the child to remain at home?
- does the trauma of family break-up and the hazards of care pose a greater risk to the child than exposure to the possibility of further abuse?

To answer the questions, social workers must understand the legal framework and case law and have a good knowledge of child development and the effects of child abuse; they must be able to make a detailed assessment of the family and evaluate what social work skills and agency resources are required to resolve the problems in a limited space of time. The Cleveland Report recognised that this is a highly skilled task that should be undertaken by well-trained and experienced staff working alongside doctors, nurses, the police and others responsible for the care of children. However, there is currently an extreme shortage of trained social workers in many parts of the country.

The Cleveland Report also recommends (see Appendix II) the development of inter-disciplinary co-operation. It says that each agency has prime responsibility for a particular aspect of the problem. Neither childrens' nor parents' needs and rights can be adequately met or protected unless agencies agree a framework for their interaction. However, the statutory duties of Social Service Departments must be recognised.

In reality other professionals are often ambivalent about how much and in what way they want to be involved in the uncomfortable issues of child protection. They themselves are overworked and often in short supply. There seems to be a tendency to assume that the need for assistance and informed advice on future plans diminishes when care begins. Yet, since the legal provisions make it difficult to place children for adoption without good evidence of parental failure, there must almost inevitably be some risk taken to obtain this either by keeping children at home or attempting rehabilitation. The alternative is long term care with all its well-documented hazards. Not surprisingly, few other professionals are familiar with the complexities of the legal framework or of the pros and cons of different forms of substitute care. The result may be that social workers have difficulty in obtaining advice in order to make informed judgements in cases where the solution always involves the weighing of risks and can be no more than the least detrimental alternative.

How much autonomy in decision-making do social workers have?

What happens if the court and social workers disagree about goals and methods of treatment?

There is an inherent limitation on social work autonomy because professional decisions about the removal of children and their committal to care have to be ratified by a court. In recent years, particularly in child sexual abuse cases, the courts have seemed increasingly critical of social work and medical recommendations and have often not followed them. Social workers have claimed that they were trying both to protect and help children whilst parents' lawyers have claimed that there was no basis of factual evidence to justify depriving parents of their children. In *C v C*, for example, a case of child sexual abuse, Hollis J[4] said:

> the conclusion she (the social worker) comes to that sexual abuse has been made out is one, however, with which I do not agree. So far as I can see, although she may have a strong impression from seeing and talking to the child that satisfies herself, it is not the type of material upon which an independent person could come to a conclusion that any case has been made out against the father.

Latey J[5] defined the problem for the courts as follows:

> there is an interface between the needs of clinical therapeutic methods and the needs of the courts in legal proceedings. In doing what has been found so far to be the best to meet the needs of the former, methods may be necessary which defeat and do not best meet the needs of the latter.

The government has now taken the argument a stage further and indicated much more forcefully that professional methods of working and decision-making have 'to be in line with the thinking of the general population'. Social workers have been reminded that they should not be resentful of outsiders' opinions 'because it is outsiders who pay our wages'.[6] The difficulty is that the Government has not so far given a clear indication of what exactly is required of social workers and how children should be protected.

What should be the main form of social services' work?

For all these reasons social workers and their managers may be ambivalent about what kind of service they want to provide and how to provide it. A child protection service implies a protective, inspectoral, controlling role for social workers, with the primary emphasis on the physical safety of the child. Before the Cleveland Report managers had often stressed this aspect of intervention. However, the Seebohm Report[7] which led to the setting up of the Social Services Departments, advocated a service to families — 'the basic aim of a social services department is to meet all the social needs of the family, or individual together as a whole'. There is a strong feeling amongst social workers, reinforced by research, that child abuse and social deprivation are linked. Child abuse, it is thought, can be reduced by providing services to families to improve or resolve their social or emotional problems.

The pressures to provide a service to families alongside a child protection service are often reflected in uncertainty about the initial intervention — is it primarily investigative or therapeutic? The former involves a more neutral approach concentrating on gathering evidence. The latter involves an attempt to establish a relationship immediately and to respond to what are thought to be the clients' feelings, or a family's patterns of relationships. The aim is to provide a different (and thereby corrective) experience or relationship which in itself offers a hope or a means of change.

The uncertainty about what to do in the face of what is usually an emotionally highly charged situation can also in part be explained by what Sheldon[8] (1987) describes as the mechanism of perceptual defence. This mechanism ensures that we do not go mad trying to examine all sensory data as if they have equally good claims on our attention. Instead he says: 'We tend to develop impressions about what should be there and look scantily to confirm that it is, rather than suspending cognitive processes while we fish for facts and subject these to logical analysis'.

The 'mental sets' that social workers develop are likely to be highly influential in determining the prior assumptions which influence social work intervention.

Sheldon[8] (1987) identified the following 'mental sets' which are often developed in training.

- Therapeutic work has much in common with psychotherapy. It is predominantly verbal exercise aimed at producing change through the generation of insight.
- In the shorter term emotional and cognitive changes produced by this process may or may not show up in the actual behaviour of individuals.
- A close confiding relationship is necessary in which the therapist has an interpretative rather than a directive role.
- The ventilation of pent-up feelings within the framework of a non-judgemental relationship will have a generally useful effect.
- In cases involving children these are best regarded as the potential beneficiaries of any useful psychological changes that can be effected in their parents.

Other 'mental sets' may be much more authoritative. The report of the Inquiry into Child Sexual Abuse in Cleveland describes the following approach:

> Child sexual abuse is essentially the misuse of power by an adult against a child: In any investigation the adult concerned is likely to misuse and exploit the power and it is difficult to carry out an effective investigation unless you are proceeding from an authoritative base ie a place of safety order.

Neither of these approaches fits easily with questions of proof, decisions about the protection and removal of children, which are in their best interests, and the Local Authority's role in bringing care proceedings. Both approaches have heightened the public concern about both the accuracy of diagnosis in child abuse—false positives *and* false negatives—and the way investigations are managed.

It seems clear that the time has come for both local authorities and social workers to define their role more clearly. This will help other organisations and professions and even society itself to clarify their own views. The Report of the Inquiry into Child Abuse in Cleveland highlighted the issues for concern and made recommendations to prevent their continuation. The government will now introduce legislation which will give parents more opportunity to challenge social work decisions in the courts. The government has also published Guidelines on Working Together for all the relevant professions. The following suggestions about the way social workers should intervene and manage child abuse are based on these reports and are in line with existing practice in some agencies.

First, it needs to be made clear that the statutory service provided is first and foremost a child protection service and that services to families are based on a recognition of this. Bentovim[9] (1987) has written an important position statement to this effect. He says, quoting Bosormenyi Nagy,[10] 'the chain of consequences point toward the interest of posterity. . . . The abused child lives in a formative present which may have lasting consequences for her future survival. Moreover, if she is lastingly affected she may have a corresponding impact on her children.' He continues that it is clear from these writings that the therapists' primary responsibility must be to the person or people most at risk in the family. This will be the child and sometimes other siblings. As Margolin[11] (1982) says 'it is the therapist's ethical responsibility to abdicate the role of relationship adviser and help a threatened person find protection.' Bentovim concludes,

> it should be possible with a family systems orientation to devise ways of working which enable us to protect the child and develop relationships with professional and legal systems to ensure a therapeutic attitude to families . . . It is possible to find ways of working effectively using family systems approaches to child abuse, eg the Rochdale group,[12] which combine the use of statutory authority and therapy.

This approach must be linked with recognition that ultimately children can only be protected on the basis of evidence that can be tested in court. It would need therefore to be linked with recognition of the importance of the initial investigative role, with an emphasis on the need for gathering evidence and making a detailed assessment before treatment begins. There would need to be at this stage more stress on establishing the facts and basing decisions on these, and less on social work intuition, and the clients' perceptions and feelings about events. More joint interviewing and closer liaison with the police would help to achieve this. Such a change would also involve a major change in emphasis on social work training courses and in the attitude of many social workers.

Secondly there must once again be more emphasis on providing a service to the whole family as envisaged in the Seebohm Report as this has been re-interpreted in the Cleveland Report. Much more emphasis is placed on the provision of information, consultation, and involvement of parents in decision-making wherever it is appropriate.

Thirdly there must be a full assessment of both child and family. The Cleveland Report emphasises that a child's needs and best interests cannot be fully considered in isolation from knowledge about, and full understanding of all the circumstances relating to its parents—their strengths and weaknesses as individuals, their functioning as a couple, their capacity as parents and the known risks which any facet of their behaviour or attitude may have for the child. Balanced judgements cannot be made without careful appraisal.

Fourthly the criteria for decision-making, planning, and the provision of treatment should be clearly targeted to the resolution of identified problems and must relate more evidently to observed behaviour and other evidence. More emphasis should be placed on the use of written reports to assist in recognising and weighing evidence, in supervision and in decision-making. This, of course, would necessitate good clerical provisions and more involvement and assistance from Legal Departments.

Fifthly social workers must have a good knowledge of child development—both physical and emotional, and greater ability to recognise signs of abuse, neglect and failure to thrive. This will also enable them to know when to call on other disciplines.

Sixthly there must be the development of more inter-agency co-operation which acknowledges the statutory responsibilities of the Social Service Department but accepts that no single agency has the pre-eminent responsibility in the assessment of child abuse. Joint training and the implementation of the DHSS draft guidelines would help to make working together and a multi-disciplinary service a reality. This would facilitate both a better service to families and more debate and more agreement about appropriate standards for good enough parenting.

Finally there must be more emphasis on offering treatment and resources once a diagnosis and a legal framework has been established. The local authority must try to offer something better to children and families as a result of their intervention.

The current reality is that many children are being protected from abusing parents. Local authorities, however, have not hitherto usually been accountable for the quality of their parenting, or their services. Some children and families have been offered a good service, but there has also been much cause for concern. An overall improvement seems unlikely without changes at all levels, especially in role definition, in training, in professional assumptions and in the provision of service. Social workers now need to agree and to make it clear that combining child protection and a service to families is a complex task which requires highly skilled professionals and a well-resourced organisation to carry it out. As the Cleveland Report concluded, social workers also need the support of the public to continue in the job the public needs them to do.

References

1. Blom Cooper, QC, L (1987). 'A child in mind'. The Report of the Commission of Inquiry into the circumstances surrounding the death of Kimberley Carlile, London Borough of Greenwich.
2. Report of the Inquiry into Child Abuse in Cleveland. Cm 412, HMSO, 1988.

3. Bentovim, A (1988). 'Working with Abusing Parents'. Paper given at the 7th International Conference of Child Abuse and Neglect.

4. C v C Child Abuse: Evidence [1987] 1FLR p 323–31.

5. Re M [1987] 1FLR p 293–6.

6. Report of speech by Health Minister, *Social Work Today*, 27 October 1988, p 3.

7. Report of the Committee on Local Authority and Allied Personal Social Services. Cmnd. 3703, HMSO.

8. Sheldon, B (1987). 'The Psychology of Incompetence' in *After Beckford, essays on themes related to child abuse*. Department of Social Policy, Royal Holloway and Bedford New College.

9. Bentovim, A (1987). Physical and sexual abuse in children— role of the family therapist. *Journal of Family Therapy*, 4.

10. Bosormenyi Nagy (1985). Commentary, transgenerational solidarity, therapists' mandate and ethics. *Family Process*, 24.

11. Margolin, G (1982). Ethical and legal considerations in marital and family therapy. *American Psychologist*, 37.

12. Dale, P et al (1985). *Dangerous Families*, Tavistock, London.

CHAPTER 4

The Cleveland Child Abuse Inquiry

ALLAN LEVY Q.C

(The following is based on a paper presented at a conference on child abuse held in Rio de Janeiro in September 1988)

In 1987 a large number of children, over a relatively short space of time, were removed from their parents in Cleveland, North East England following allegations that the children had been sexually abused.

The allegations were, to a significant extent, based upon a controversial medical test relating to physical signs of sexual abuse — reflex anal dilatation.

There were considerable delays in the cases coming to court and there was great concern about the medical, social work, and legal procedures and practices adopted.

In July 1987 the United Kingdom government ordered that a Judicial Inquiry should take place to examine the arrangements for dealing with suspected cases of child abuse, including in particular, child sexual abuse in Cleveland. This involved a searching examination of what occurred between January and July 1987.

Cleveland is not a very well known area. When the matter became known to the media, one radio station in London thought that the events were taking place in Cleveland, Ohio in the United States.

The Inquiry, which lasted 74 days between August 1987 and January 1988, was held in Middlesbrough which is typical perhaps of the area : known for its high unemployment and its football team.

The judge who conducted the Inquiry, Mrs Justice Butler-Sloss, (who has since become a Court of Appeal judge) quickly realised that she had to deal with a large number of complex and varied matters which were not unique to Cleveland. Accordingly, her findings are of much wider application, being relevant to other parts of the United Kingdom and perhaps other countries.

I can only deal here with some aspects of the Inquiry. I have, of necessity, to simplify to some extent what were very complex issues. The Report of the Inquiry runs to 320 pages (Cm 412, HMSO, 1988).

The background

What led to the exceptional necessity for the setting up of a Judicial Inquiry?

On the 1st January 1987, a consultant paediatrician, Dr Higgs, took up her appointment in Cleveland. She had a particular interest in the diagnosis and treatment of child sexual abuse. She linked up with another paediatrician, Dr Wyatt who was already working in Cleveland.

Soon after her arrival Dr Higgs made contact with the social services department and joined in various multi-disciplinary and community projects.

Ultimately the Report prepared by the judge said (at page 13) that, 'in general we were satisfied with the arrangements and the inter-disciplinary working of the main agencies in Cleveland in their response to child abuse other than child sexual abuse.' It was, however, the diagnosis of sexual abuse by Drs Higgs and Wyatt, and the consequences of those diagnoses, which was to cause great controversy for many months.

Between them, Dr Higgs and Dr Wyatt, diagnosed sexual abuse in 121 children from 57 families in a period of 5 months in the first half of 1987. An additional 4 cases were diagnosed by other doctors. A high percentage of the diagnoses were made in June and July 1987.

Central to the controversial diagnoses of the doctors was diagnosis of anal abuse by a test known as reflex anal dilatation. Another and more descriptive name is the 'buttock separation test'. The signs of habitual anal abuse were a central issue in the Inquiry. Medical opinion as to the validity of the reflex anal dilatation test in diagnosing anal abuse was divided and the media took up the controversy with great enthusiasm and not a little inaccuracy.

The number of cases diagnosed by the doctors in Cleveland over a period of 5 months bore no comparison to any previous comparable period. They were disturbing by any standards. A serious crisis then developed for the following main reasons:

Firstly, the medical test used by Drs Higgs and Wyatt was not accepted by other influential doctors who thought their diagnoses mistaken. In particular, doctors used by the police—whose role was to look for evidence in the criminal as opposed to civil context—became strongly opposed to Drs Higgs and Wyatt. Co-operation broke down. The police withdrew from their multi-disciplinary role and took up an entrenched position.

Secondly, the sheer numbers of children involved meant that the social services department could not cope: their resources in effect collapsed. Ultimately, some children were placed in Middles-brough's General Hospital where there were some unpleasant scenes involving distressed children and protesting parents. From March 1987 to July 1987, 104 children suspected of having been sexually abused were removed from their homes and admitted to the hospital. In the whole of 1986 there were 2 such children.

Thirdly, the social workers placed unquestioning confidence in the medical diagnoses of Drs Higgs and Wyatt with the result that there was no real attempt to assess the families before children were taken from their homes on the authority of hastily obtained emergency court orders. The most used order was a Place of Safety Order. It is designed to give emergency protection to a child who is considered to be at risk by a magistrate. Application is usually made by a social worker or by the police. Parents are not informed in advance and the child may be taken to a place of safety for up to 28 days. Full records were not kept by the social workers or the court of the orders made. Further the parents were not allowed access to their children in many of the cases so that so-called 'dis-closure work' could be carried out: that is the interviewing of the child with a view to discovering by, for example, question and answer or the use of anatomically correct dolls, the nature and extent of the sexual abuse. It would appear that no considera-tion was given to the possible removal of the alleged abuser as opposed to the child.

Fourthly, the social services department failed to take proper legal advice until far too late. Between April and June 1987 a local authority lawyer was present at only 3 out of 175 case conferences.

Fifthly, there was a crisis in the court system as a result of the number of cases requiring hearing.

The effect of the taking of a child from the family home and the denial of access naturally brought strong reactions from parents who were initially isolated but who gradually organised themselves over a period of time. They obtained lawyers and the vehement support of a particularly articulate member of the British Parliament who raised the matter in the House of Commons. In addition they gained the very powerful support of a large section of the media. What was happening in Cleveland—the large number of cases, the questioning of the accuracy of the diagnoses and the role of the social workers and the police, and the distress and alarm of the parents—became national and eventually international news. It became necessary for a highly respected judge to look into the situation.

Two matters should be emphasised. Firstly, although the judge was very critical indeed of many aspects of what occurred in Cleveland, she discounted all allegations of impropriety or of conspiracies. She considered that everyone meant well, but many were misguided.

Secondly, the Inquiry Report did not rule upon the individual cases as to the accuracy or otherwise of the actual diagnoses. A number of the children, because of the importance and difficulty of the issues, became wards of the English High Court as opposed to having their cases dealt with in local juvenile courts before magistrates. In fact 67 out of 125 children became wards. Of the 121 children diagnosed by Drs Higgs and Wyatt 98 are now back at home with their parents. Some of the returns are subject to conditions which include supervision orders on the children and medical examinations in respect of them. The actual number of accurate diagnoses may well be a matter of speculation well into the future.

The Report of the judge dealt in the main with the management of suspected child sexual abuse cases. To the surprise of some, it did not rule on the merits of the actual diagnoses.

Conclusions and recommendations

There are many conclusions and recommendations (see Appendix II) in the Report which will be of considerable interest to, for example, the medical, legal and social work professions and to law enforcement agencies. The following may be of particular interest.

The judge observed (Inquiry Report, p 243) that it was entirely proper for the two paediatricians to play their part in the identification of sexual abuse in children referred to them. They were responsible for the care of their patients. Nonetheless they had a responsibility to examine their own actions: to consider whether their practice was always correct and whether it was in the best interests of the children. They are to be criticised for not doing so and for the over-confidence with which they pursued the detection of sexual abuse in children referred to them. They were not solely nor indeed principally responsible for the subsequent management of the children concerned. However the certainty of their findings in relation to children diagnosed by them without prior complaint posed particular problems for the police and social services.

The Report notes that, 'it is however important to bear in mind that those who have a responsibility to protect children at risk, such as social workers, health visitors, police and doctors have in the past been criticised for failure to act in sufficient time and to take adequate steps to protect children who are being damaged. In Cleveland the general criticism by the public has been of over-enthusiasm and zeal in the actions taken. It is difficult for professionals to balance the conflicting interests and needs in the enormously important and delicate field of child sexual abuse. We hope that professionals will not as a result of the Cleveland experience stand back and hesitate to act to protect the children.' (Inquiry Report, p 244)

As far as specific recommendations are concerned, the following are important examples:

(a) There is a need to recognise and describe the extent of the problem of child sexual abuse and to receive more accurate data of the abuse which is identified;

(b) There is a danger that in looking to the welfare of the children believed to be the victims of sexual abuse the children themselves may be overlooked. The child is a person and not an object of concern;

(c) Professionals should always listen carefully to what the child has to say and take seriously what is said;

(d) Children should not be subjected to repeated medical examinations solely for evidential purposes and should not be subjected to repeated interviews nor to the probing and confrontational type of 'disclosure' interview for the same purpose;

(e) The police should develop and practise inter-agency working, including joint planning and interviews of children in investigation of sexual abuse within the family or caring agency;

(f) The medical profession should investigate the natural history and the significance of signs and symptoms which may be associated with child sexual abuse. Consideration should be given to inquiring into the significance of the phenomenon of anal dilatation. (The judge was satisfied from the evidence that the consensus is that the sign of anal dilatation is abnormal and suspicious and requires further investigation. It is not in itself evidence of anal abuse);

(g) Specialist Assessment Teams should be established consisting of an approved medical practitioner, a senior social worker, and a police officer with sufficient authority to co-ordinate the investigation of cases. Their function is to undertake a full multi-disciplinary assessment of the child and the family in cases of particular difficulty;

(h) Training is one of the major needs shown by the Cleveland experience. It applies to each profession. All lawyers, for instance, engaged in this type of work including Judges and Magistrates should have a greater awareness and inform themselves about the nature of child abuse and the management of children subjected to abuse and in particular sexual abuse.

Importance of Cleveland

The events in Cleveland are important for many reasons:

- They emphasise the significance of not allowing a rush to judgement in suspected child sexual abuse cases;
- They underline the need for a genuinely multi-disciplinary approach to problems;
- They illustrate the need for careful informed assessment by the professionals involved;
- They point the way for doctors, social workers and lawyers, amongst others, to re-examine their views and methods, and also to re-examine the training they receive.

One thing is quite apparent. The subject of child sexual abuse in the United Kingdom will never be the same again following the events in Cleveland in the early months of 1987.

CHAPTER 5

Communicating with Children – Communicating with the Court

MARGERY BRAY

Social work consultant

Decisions affecting children's lives are arguably the most important ever to be taken in a court of law for they are often life changing in nature having profound impact on a life which in many cases has hardly begun, and upon a human being who is often powerless to influence the outcome. In situations such as these surely it must be incumbent upon all of us who have a professional involvement in this process to use the very best of our skills, knowledge and experience to help to get the decision as right as possible.

Yet we live in an adult world. We organise our institutions and our decision-making processes for our convenience. Our courts are adult arenas. We use adult language to communicate subtle ideas and constructs. In our dealings with children we learn to advise, control and direct them. And often our approach to decision-making in respect of them bases itself upon the view that children are fundamentally unreliable in their ability to contribute to the process.

The brutal reality seems to be that in a society where traditionally children must be 'seen and not heard', the message of the Cleveland Inquiry of 'Listening to Children', of a 'Child being a person and not an object of concern', of an expectation placed upon adults to 'Explain to children what is going on' and 'Have their views and wishes placed before the court', must surely herald a fundamental shift in our thinking and attitudes towards children for, as professionals, we are faced with the prospect of being asked to modify our practice and make both ourselves and the legal process relevant to the child. In whatever profession we belong it is unlikely that our training has equipped us to communicate with children, for communicating *about* children is what we have learned to do—communicating *with* them is a new area for many of us.

So how may we go about the process of making contact with a child in this context and how do we provide the purest possible channel of communication between a child's world and the other adult or adults who may never have the opportunity to meet the child, and upon whose shoulders rests the responsibility for the decision?

In keeping with many other professionals in the difficult field of child abuse we have, at SACCS (Sexual Abuse : Child Consultancy Service), been wrestling with some of these issues for some time. The following ideas are culled from a model of practice which we have evolved over a period of time working with many different children in varying circumstances in courts throughout the country.

A child focused v adult dominated context

The Medium

We believe that the medium in which any talking is done with the child needs to be child focused as opposed to adult dominated. Very often this environment is not readily available. We create it by carrying equipment, toys and other play materials which immediately create an ambience where the child feels more at home with familiar objects which make some connection with his or her world.

So often, as adults in our dealings with children, we act and interact with them in a way that is familiar to us. We sit children on chairs and talk to, at, or with them. We do this for our own convenience as it is the medium in which we are most familiar—we forget how we felt as children. In the 'Seen and not heard' climate which prevailed when we were children, many of us were seldom listened to ourselves.

The Language

As adults, often without thinking, we use language with which we are familiar but for which the child has no frame of reference— 'case conference', 'witness box', 'care order', even the word 'court'. We say things to children such as, 'Now Laura, I understand you are subject to a supervision order under the matrimonial causes rules' without taking into account the cognitive abilities of the child we are talking to. Talking children's language is a skill which some of us find particularly difficult to master; it causes us discomfort and embarrassment. In child abuse cases this is complicated by the fact that the subject under discussion is very often embarrassing and distressing, both for the child and for the interviewer.

Using children's language to make self relevant

Who is this person? What is she doing here? Why is she sitting talking to me? These are all questions in a child's mind unless the adult takes time to explain the function of his or her role at the very beginning. It is of crucial importance that the adult uses children's language to make him or herself relevant and understood, and simplifies both the tasks ahead and the process, in a way in which the child can understand. A typical conversation might be as follows:

'I bet you're wondering what I'm doing here?'
'Yes.'
'Well, my name's Kate Banks. You know how some people live with just their mummies?'
'Yes.'
'Do you have any friends who live with just their mummies?'
Nods . . . 'Melissa.'
'Oh, I see, Melissa.'
'And do you know some children who live with just their daddies? Can you think of anyone in your class who does that?'
'Yes, Ray Brown.'
'Okay. And some children live with their mummies and daddies, don't they?'
'Yep.'
'And other children don't live with either their mummies or their daddies, do they? They live with other people's mummies and daddies?'
'In foster, like me?'
'Yes, a bit like you, because you live with Uncle John and Auntie Sarah, don't you? and they're Anna's mummy and daddy, aren't

they? And you know, when children don't live with their mummies and daddies and live somewhere else with another mummy and daddy, sometimes a wise person (or wise people) have to decide what should happen. The wise person wants to try to get things right for the little boy. The wise person knows that I spend a lot of time with children and like talking to them and being with them. His office rang me up last week and asked if I could come and spend some time with Mathew, and ask him if he could help the grown-ups to try and get things right for him. Do you think Mathew would be able to help him to understand what had happened? What do you think the wise person will need to know which might help him to decide?'

The focus of the task becomes the collection of information which the child thinks the wise person would need to know. We may look at pictures of judges so that Mathew begins to understand what judges are and what they do. We also carry a model court in which the child can place figures which we can also use to help enable him to understand where the decisions are likely to be taking place and who the actors in the piece are.

We might ponder over information, the information which the wise person might need to know, such as what are the sad things that have happened to the little boy, why he thinks he came to be living here, or what he thinks should happen now.

Depending perhaps upon the nature of the enquiry we may be looking gently to explore, through drawing, how people get angry with each other in Mathew's house, or what happens in bad dreams, or what people do to show that they love each other in Mathew's house. The focus becomes one of allowing the adult to provide a channel through which the child can communicate in the decision-making process as clearly as possible.

In child abuse enquiries there is an inevitable pressure upon the interviewer to elicit information quickly and efficiently. There are times when adult anxiety to fulfil this task overtakes sound common sense in approaches to children. There can often be a temptation to cover zealously preconceived ground in the interview without waiting to work at the child's pace. In other words, the adult agenda predominates and the information on the child's agenda is not heard.

During the early stages of the interview, therefore, we would want to switch off the adult agenda, switching onto the child's by allowing the child to explore the toys and establishing rapport. Gradually, then, the adult can begin to explore the subject area. Child sexual abuse enquiries are often influenced by the fact that sexual abuse within families is a syndrome of secrecy and denial. There are occasions when it is clear that children are simply not free to offer information because they fear it is not safe enough to do so. The provision of safety to enable the child to feel safe under those circumstances is a skilled and sensitive task and may require further exploration through play. In situations such as these, in our experience, over-zealous attempts to elicit information from children inevitably force a further retreat into silence and reinforce fear and anxiety.

In the presentation of evidence in court, what must surely be important is that the information is presented from the child as clearly as possible. What the child said is crucial, whether said directly : 'My Uncle Roger locks me in the coal shed' or by a drawing : 'This is a picture of me in a coal shed and it's all dark and Uncle Roger says I can't come out until I'm a good boy.' One of the values of children's art is that it is tangible proof to the child that the wise person will be able to see and consider and take into account a direct contribution from the child, although clearly he will need to consider this in the light of everyone else's muddle. 'Muddles' is a concept which has meaning and relevance to children and part of the process may also be to help the child identify what the mummy's muddle might be, and the daddy's muddle, and the policeman's muddle, and the nanny's muddle, and the social worker's muddle and, as importantly, the little boy's muddle, because the judge has to hear what everybody's muddle is before he can decide how he might be able to get it right. For any opinion, regardless of how expert it may be, based on an interpretation of what the child may mean, either in play or observation of behaviour, is arguably both dangerous and riddled with the potential for inaccuracy.

Much recent attention has been focused in cases of child sexual abuse upon two different 'tools' which provide a bridge between the adult world and the child's experience. These are the use of video taping and the use of anatomically complete dolls in interviews with children.

Video taping

Many courts have insisted recently upon the video taping of interviews with children in order to scrutinise the methods used to obtain information. In this respect video is undoubtedly invaluable. Arguably, however, the use of video can only be of benefit if the end result is of sufficient quality to enable scrutiny to take place and orders for video taping of children's interviews need to take cognisance of the availability of suitable local facilities in which evidentially sound interviewing can take place.

This must surely have resource implications and as yet many local authorities have not addressed this issue. In many areas such facilities simply do not exist. Although the use of video may have much to commend it in enabling adults to form opinions on the information it yields, it is less easy to justify if one sees its use through the eyes of a child, for the process of obtaining such information from children is a delicate and sensitive one. The child, often tentative and fearful, uncertain about adult responses or the consequences of disclosing information, desperately seeks reassurance and approval, and the inhibiting presence of a video camera often adds yet another obstacle. Adults may wish to imagine the embarrassing mixture of emotions if they themselves were suddenly asked to share intimate details of their sex lives. Imagine how much more difficult this might be if the whole thing were to be video taped. Through the eyes of a child then the video camera must surely often be seen as yet another inhibiting factor.

The use of anatomically complete dolls

The debate over the use of anatomically complete dolls has often been heated. There are those who for reasons which are not obviously apparent view them as obscene, and there are claims that children find them frightening. In our experience, although caution and sensitivity need to be applied to their use, the dolls can be of great assistance to children in expressing information which often is of great relevance to the adult but holds little meaning for the child. One must not forget that when children are engaged in deviant sexual activity with adults their innocence of sexual matters divests their experiences of meaning for them. In relating such activities they, therefore, do not have a framework upon which to hang their experiences and struggle to express information which although very real in content, is devoid of meaning. Under such circumstances the dolls can enable children to bring their experiences from the abstract to the concrete. 'I can marry dad in the bath', a comment from a 4-year-old engaging in indiscriminate sexual activity is given relevance and meaning to the adult interviewer when, with the help of the dolls, the child goes on to demonstrate how 'marrying' happens. A process of clarification and elucidation takes place which gives shape and form to concepts which the child struggles to express. The dolls provide an invaluable bridge for the child's world into the adult one, and a confusing experience is shared. Part of the adult skill must then be to collect this information in such a way as to ensure that it is uncontaminated by preconception, pressure or distortion, and place it intact before the adult decision-making process.

A difficult task

Listening to children can surely only be one part of the jigsaw ; believing that they may have the ability to express what has happened to them is undoubtedly another. Finding ways as adults to help them accomplish that task is yet another. Perhaps one of the most difficult tasks facing those of us who deal professionally with abused children is the challenge of making it possible for the child to communicate that information as directly as possible to the decision-making process. Arguably, the quality of the decision which a court may take in any child's life will depend largely upon the quality of information which comes before it, and the more accurately that information reflects the child's true situation and what it is like to be that child, the closer it must surely approach getting it right for a small person rather than dealing with an 'object of concern'.

CHAPTER 6

Interviewing Children: Psychiatric Aspects

DR STEPHEN WOLKIND
Consultant child psychiatrist

It is clearly not feasible in a brief contribution to give any form of guidance as to how one should or should not interview children in particular those who may have been abused. An excellent account is available (Jones and McQuiston (1988))[1] but of course, reading must be combined with discussion with experienced practitioners and with supervision. By looking, however, at the nature of the psychiatric techniques of interviewing and at the way in which we assess children, one is compelled to go beyond a technical exercise. Inevitably it leads to the purpose of the interview and to the role of child psychiatrists in the field of abuse and to what might be expected of them when they give evidence in courts of law. I will attempt to look at the psychiatric process, at the diagnostic systems we use, at the psychiatric indicators of sexual abuse and at the way we use the concept of emotional abuse.

It is often assumed that a major role of the psychiatrist is to use his or her skills to determine 'the truth'. Hollywood and on occasion real life, have shown psychiatrists using depth or hypnotic techniques to enable a 'patient' to confess to a murder or rediscover other lost memories. Such an approach might seem ideal to help a child who is repressing unpleasant experiences or who lacks the vocabulary to describe how he or she might have been abused. It is, however, an unreal task to expect of a doctor and despite the problems over the validity of the techniques used, it poses real ethical dilemmas. The prime task of the child psychiatrist and the function of the psychiatric interview is, in fact, the same as the investigation carried out by any other doctor, namely to determine whether the patient has an illness or disorder. The need to determine in absolute terms how much of a child's story is fantasy and how much the absolute truth is of only secondary importance. I recently saw a depressed and miserable 7-year-old boy. He told me in great detail how his stepmother always put salt instead of sugar on his breakfast cereal. This had probably happened on one occasion but the actual reality was of far less interest to me than the fact that this child had chosen to tell me this story in a tone which seemed to mix anger and despair. By concentrating on this aspect of the child's contributions I was avoiding a very great dilemma which seems to have often bedevilled psychiatry — can you believe all that your patients tell you?

Freud during the 1880s became convinced that he had discovered the prime cause of adult neurotic illness when he found that his predominantly female patients would, with alarming predictability, describe scenes of seduction usually performed by fathers. Later, after attempting and failing to obtain confirmatory details from other family members, he decided that these statements must have been fantasies and it was in the structure of the fantasies that lay the origins of the later illness. The debate about the relative importance of early life events in the genesis of psychiatric illness has continued over the years. With Freud's patients it is possible that some of their accounts were fantasies but that some, perhaps even the majority, had indeed been sexually abused as children. What Freud was probably correct about, however, was that at that later stage it was the telling of the story which was of more importance than what had actually happened. This attitude to an individual's account is of course in marked contrast to the expectations that others in different professions would have about their interviews. For police and to a lesser extent social workers, determining whether a child's story is true must be the first priority.

Over the last few years this distinction between psychiatric and other interviews had tended to become somewhat blurred. It gradually became apparent to a small number of professionals including child psychiatrists, that sexual abuse of children was not a rare event but a common experience particularly among those being referred to clinics with behavioural and emotional disorders. The task of determining the details of what had happened and presenting these to courts, in order to prevent a recurrence, became for these doctors a major priority. The difficulty was that many of the patients were too young, too disturbed or too developmentally delayed to give a coherent account of what had happened to them.

To deal with this situation a variety of techniques were adapted to help create investigative interviews. The word adapted rather than developed seems appropriate, for the techniques such as hypothetical and alternate questioning, discussed in some detail in the Cleveland Report, were not new innovations but ones well established and of accepted value in the psychiatric treatment of children and families. In this latter situation where the relationship between the patient and therapist is of major importance, the use of a hypothetical question such as 'and if you have really burnt the house down what might have happened to all the family', could enable a child to open out about fears and angry feelings which might otherwise have been difficult or impossible to illicit. However, to use a question such as 'but if daddy *had* touched you down below, what would you have thought', after a child had replied 'no' when being asked if she had been touched is very different. It could be legitimate if this was part of treatment after other definite evidence has proved that the child had indeed been abused by her father. It is far more problematic if it is being used to obtain factual information when there is doubt about whether the abuse had occurred. Disagreements on this point split the profession and child psychiatrists are probably secretly relieved that it was a paediatric rather than a psychiatric technique which suddenly became front-page news. The Cleveland Report suggests considerable caution be applied to the use of such approaches and equally over the use of sexually explicit dolls as a way of obtaining information. What was particularly worrying about some of the pre-Cleveland interviewing is that these special techniques with all their limitations were used with very disturbed children instead of, rather than in addition to, the full psychiatric assessment.

The diagnostic process

After these cautionary statements it is necessary to explore in more detail what a child psychiatrist can positively contribute to social service departments and courts who are deciding the future of a child. As described above, the prime task is to establish whether or not a psychiatric disorder is present. Following this a number of subsidiary questions arise. If the answer is yes, what is the nature of that disorder, what impact is it having on the life of the child, is it linked to associated or developmental or learning difficulties, what might be its cause and its prognosis and what, if any, treatment is required? This emphasis on what might appear to be a very traditional medical approach might cause some surprise to lawyers and social workers who expect from a psychiatrist not a diagnosis but general advice on how a child's needs could be best met; for example, should a child be removed from it's family for adoption or is re-habilitation to it's parents feasible. To make a decision in such a case a court will have to weigh up a great number of social and legal factors. What the child psychiatrist can contribute using his diagnostic model is what impact any decision might have on a child's psychiatric state. Might a disorder improve after adoption. In a child with no disorder, might one develop were he or she to be removed from home. In both cases what might be the long term prognosis of the disorder. The amount of empirical research in developmental psychopathology and child psychiatry is now sufficient to enable child psychiatrists to give estimates of the probability of changes occurring in a child. The possible effects of a particular course of action on a child's psychiatric state will not in itself determine whether or not that course should be followed but it can offer helpful information which should be included in the decision-making process.

If this diagnostic approach is followed a major advantage is the very comprehensive assessment of the child that it involves. The diagnostic system used follows World Health Organisation criteria and is internationally recognised.

Much work has been done on the reliability and the validity of the various categories in the scheme. To make a diagnosis involves systematic interviewing of the child, the parents and usually the family together. Because children can behave totally differently in different settings, school and other relevant reports are required. The diagnosis made at the end of this process is a complex one.

Sufficient information must be obtained to describe the child on five different dimensions or axes. The first is the actual psychiatric disorder. Its importance to those making decisions about children is considerable. Certain disorders such as those concerning a child's conduct are primarily environmentally caused. A child with such difficulties has a poor outlook for mature development if he or she continues in an environment which is maintaining that disorder. In a different setting the outlook could be quite different. With other conditions such as an attention deficit disorder, improvement might not necessarily occur with a change of environment.

The next three axes cover the child's intellectual, developmental and physical status. Too often so much attention is paid to whether a child has or has not been abused that crucial questions about health and educational needs are not asked. The final axis deals with associated environmental and family factors. It is in this axis that abuse whether physical, emotional or sexual will be rated. These are in themselves not diagnoses but factors which might explain why a disorder commenced or failed to improve. It is worth re-emphasising that sexual abuse is not a psychiatric diagnosis but a possible cause of a psychiatric disorder. This is not a question of semantics but of very great practical importance. Sexual abuse can be followed by a great range of consequences from minor anxiety states to severe depression, from slight stroppiness to severe and dangerous aggression. The sexual abuse per se is usually of less importance than the seriously disturbed relationship that it symbolises. The needs of any abused child would be better recognised from the overall psychiatric picture than from the fact that he or she has been sexually abused. It should be of concern that there has been a tendency to see sexual abuse as a homogeneous concept which requires special projects devoted to its treatment.

The needs of a sexually abused, mentally retarded child with physical failure to thrive and gross hyper-activity are quite different from those of a child with good academic abilities and high self-esteem who is understandably depressed by the betrayal of trust by a stepfather.

Psychiatric indicators of sexual abuse

The two cases mentioned above illustrate how differently children who have been sexually abused can present to psychiatrists. They also should help us realise that in looking at any psychiatric disorder, there is only extremely rarely a single cause. In looking for causes we are guided by research which has demonstrated the way a variety of innate and environmental factors contribute to the final picture. Examples of an innate factor in the child could be a particular constellation of temperamental characteristics which many parents would find hard to cope with or cognitive deficits which make it hard for the child to understand the world around it and the social rules which govern it. Environmental factors would include continuing disharmony between parents, which can be devastating for the child or unreal expectations by the child's school. The developments of recent years, the Cleveland Inquiry and the advice of the DHSS now confirm that to this list (which should be considered routinely in all cases by child psychiatrists) should be added sexual abuse. The DHSS Diagnosis of Child Sexual Abuse : Guidance for Doctors[2] emphasises the wide variety of signs and symptoms that might be caused at least in part by sexual abuse. Some, such as clear descriptions by the child, should give rise to severe suspicion, in others, such as unexplained changes in behaviour, suicidal gestures or running away, the suspicion should be mild or moderate. In any cases where there are not clear reasons why the disorder has commenced, sexual abuse must always be considered.

Emotional abuse

A point which causes a great deal of concern to child psychiatrists is the rather doubtful attitude of the legal profession to emotional abuse. The X-ray corroboration of a broken bone caused by a blow from a violent parent or physical signs of clear sexual abuse are almost gratefully received as clear evidence which will have a major impact on decision-making. In practice the physical traumata of abuse will in most cases heal within a relatively brief period and leave only minor scars. In contrast, the emotional abuse which accompanies these injuries or which more often is inflicted in the absence of physical damage can have profound effects on the individual for the rest of his or her life. The difficulty, however, is in defining emotional abuse and in deciding when this is sufficiently harmful to warrant legal intervention. Almost any type of parenting behaviour, such as giving too little spending money, or preventing a child from sucking it's thumb, could in theory be taken by some as evidence of emotional abuse. The need is to try to restrict this down and find a set of criteria which do require intervention. Here again the psychiatric assessment can be of help.

Clearly a first point must be evidence of grossly abnormal parenting of a quality which is outside the acceptable and wide range normally seen. Examples would be a total absence of any positive affirmation of the child or sets of expectations which no child could reach. This must be accompanied, however, by the presence in the child of a psychiatric disorder which is known to be largely caused by environmental factors and which has a poor prognosis for later development. Insistence on this point can upset social workers confronted by examples of totally neglectful parenting. If the child is not showing evidence of a disorder there may be very strong social reasons for intervening but this cannot be thought of as emotional abuse. One might disapprove of particular patterns of family life but the absence of an obvious psychiatric disorder in the child should lead to very considerable caution. The third point is that in addition to the presence of the two criteria described so far there must be the refusal or inability of the parents to use or accept appropriate intervention. I deliberately say appropriate because too often the type of intervention offered is designed to meet the needs of the therapist rather than the family. Further discussion of these different criteria have been presented elsewhere (Wolkind (1988)).[3]

Why I have ended with this brief account of emotional abuse is that it brings together well the very real contribution child psychiatric interviewing techniques can make in assessing the needs of children. The more the child psychiatrist keeps to his traditional role of obtaining a full psychiatric history with a view to diagnosing a disorder, the more use his findings will be to those who have to decide the future of children.

References

1. Jones and McQuiston (1988). *Interviewing the Sexually Abused Child*. Gaskell and Royal College of Psychiatrists, London.
2. DHSS (1988). Diagnosis of Child Sexual Abuse : Guidance for Doctors. HMSO, London.
3. Wolkind, S. (1988). Emotional signs. *Journal* SWL 2, 88.

CHAPTER 7

Dolls as an Aid to Interviewing Children: A Legal View

SEÁN ENRIGHT
Barrister

We are primarily concerned here with the use of anatomically correct dolls as a diagnostic aid in the detection of sexual abuse of young children. Readers may feel, however, that the principles governing the conduct of interviews utilising anatomically correct dolls have an application to interviewing children in general. Interview techniques incorporating the use of anatomically correct dolls have been developed at The Hospital for Sick Children at Great Ormond Street in recent years. The interview techniques are well known. Suffice it to say at this stage that the dolls have been used both as a therapy aid in treating children who have been abused and as a means of diagnosing whether abuse has taken place.

Differing perspectives

It is generally accepted that the use of these dolls as a therapeutic or diagnostic aid is still in the experimental stage. Indeed, the use of dolls has been a matter of considerable controversy (see for instance, *The Report of the Inquiry into Child Abuse in Cleveland*, Cm 412, HMSO 1988 Chapter 12 paragraphs 54 to 64 inclusive[1]). A number of the judiciary have expressed strong views on the use of the dolls in such interviews. In *Re N* [1987] 1 FLR 280[2] Swinton Thomas J said that:

> The interview technique was still in its experimental stages and the court had reservations as to whether the truth was necessarily elicited.

In *C v C* [1987] 1 FLR 321, Hollis J expressed 'grave disquiet' over the use of dolls.

In fact judicial reaction has been mixed. And in the light of judicial advice (notably from Latey J in *Re M* [1987] 1 FLR 293) clinicians at Great Ormond Street have refined and modified the interview technique. They have also defended and developed their ideas at length in various periodicals (see for instance Bentovim, Tranter and Vizard[3]).

This chapter, however, is written from the perspective of a lawyer (and a parents' lawyer at that). There follows a number of criticisms of the interview technique. However, one would preface these criticisms and reservations by accepting a number of propositions. First, many abused children find it very difficult to talk of their plight through fear or feelings of guilt or simply a lack of the necessary vocabulary. Secondly, the dolls (in properly trained hands) have helped many children to 'unburden' themselves and have, on occasion, assisted in the diagnosis of abuse. Thirdly, that the clinicians at Great Ormond Street and elsewhere have responded to criticism and have made efforts to eradicate more objectionable features of the system (such as the use of leading and hypothetical questions). Fourthly, it is now broadly accepted that clinicians ought to approach interviews with an open mind as to whether abuse has taken place or not. So the very real reservations and criticisms of the technique expressed below are not to be taken as lightly dismissing the skills and dedication of those involved in the detection of child abuse.

Interview techniques

There is no such thing as a definitively correct interview. So much depends on clinical judgements and an ability to relate to and respond to a child. Techniques of interviewing differ from institution to institution and indeed from clinician to clinician. Although many institutions have taken a lead from The Great Ormond Street Child Sexual Abuse Team.

It is difficult to lay down any hard and fast rules. Diagnostic interviews, however, should follow a fairly distinct structure. Ideally, the interviewer and child will already be acquainted. There will be a settling in period. The child will then be introduced to the dolls which are fully clothed. The child is then encouraged to undress the dolls and to name (using its own words) the various sexual organs. The way is then open for the interviewer to encourage the child to disclose abuse using 'play as a medium for communication' (see Bentovim et al[3]).

Within this framework much depends on the individual child and on the skill of the interviewer.

Again one would reiterate that we are not concerned with the majority of interviews where the abuse has already been established. In such cases interviews are for therapeutic purposes.

We are concerned with a second and smaller category of children who are suspected of being victims of abuse. Often in such cases, there is no supporting medical evidence. The reasons for referral in such cases range from the abuse of a sibling or the existence of a cluster of secondary symptoms which have given rise to concern. Such secondary symptoms might include bedwetting, failure to thrive, sexual precociousness and unduly sexual play.

This category of child who is then interviewed with the aid of dolls is most at risk of an erroneous diagnosis of abuse or indeed a 'false negative' finding. It is with this in mind that we can turn our attention to some questionable assumptions which under-pin the use of the dolls. We will also look at some objectionable features of the practical application of these interviewing techniques.

Some questionable assumptions

The desirability and efficacy of the interview techniques

It is fundamentally important to remember that the interview technique is still in the experimental stage. Indeed there is a considerable body of medical and legal opinion which remains deeply sceptical. One practitioner expressed this body of opinion in these blunt terms: 'it should be unethical to use this technique in the case of non admitted child abuse' (Dr Connell in evidence: *Re N* [1987] 1 FLR 280, at p 288A).

This view was echoed by Hollis J in *C v C* [1987] 1 FLR 321, at p 330. The judge indicated that he was 'not at all satisfied that such diagnostic interviews were in the best interests of any child, except possibly where the sexual abuse had already been proven.'

The rationale for this view is twofold. First, the method of interviewing may not elicit reliable information. Secondly, 'the investigative procedure may itself be sexualising and abusive' (see Cleveland Inquiry Report, para 12.30[1]).

Introducing children to the dolls

If one accepts the desirability of undertaking such interviews, there is then a considerable amount of controversy as to when the child should be introduced to the dolls.

There are two questions to be considered. First, at what stage in an investigation into alleged abuse against a child ought these dolls to be employed? There has been a tendency for some agencies to employ these dolls at the outset of an investigation. It is now clear that this ought not to happen. The Cleveland Inquiry Report concluded that the dolls 'should not be used as the first stage method of evaluation' (para 12.58[1]) and that: 'Their use seems highly undesirable as a routine prop in initial interviews'.

The second question arises once a decision has been made to use anatomically correct dolls in a particular investigation. It is this: once clinician and child have met, how soon can the child be introduced to the dolls? This is a much more vexed question. Much depends on the interviewer's judgement of the child's situation. It may be imperative that a diagnosis be made urgently or the interviewer may form the view that the child has an overwhelming need for immediate therapy.

The counter view is that a child ought to have time to get to know the interviewer as a person. There might be one or two interviews before the dolls are produced. Certainly a child ought never to be introduced to the dolls by an interviewer who is effectively a stranger.

That sexualised play with or aversion to anatomically correct dolls indicates abuse

The consensus of medical opinion is that aversion to the dolls or sexualised play with the dolls is indicative of abuse having taken place, although it is widely accepted that these indications are not definitive. Indeed, there is evidence that some non-abused children engage in sexual play with these dolls (Dr Cameron in evidence to Cleveland Inquiry: see Cleveland Report, para 12.60[1]).

One would accept, of course, that the experience of the medical profession suggests that aversion to dolls or sexualised play with dolls is an indicator of abuse. It is, however, too early to know what weight should be attached to these factors. Nothing can be taken on trust. Indeed, Bentovim et al[3] accept that 'there is a dearth of adequate research material to guide us about behaviour of ordinary non abused children with diagnostic aids such as the anatomically correct dolls' (p 23).

There have been studies on this point but one of the main difficulties is building up a comparative base of non-abused children. How can any researcher know that all of the children in the comparative study are non-abused?

The practical application of the technique – some objectionable features

Although the concept of disclosure through play is attractive and has been subject to continual refinement and modification, the practial application often falls far short of the theory. It is worth looking at some of the problems.

Preconception of abuse

An interviewer who harbours a preconception that abuse has taken place, runs the risk of rendering the entire interview worthless in terms of any evidential weight which a court might otherwise attach. Regrettably, however, although the need to approach an interview with an open mind has been widely publicised, the lesson still has not permeated through to all levels. The necessity for objectivity has been well illustrated by Dr David Paul :[4]

> In the case of very young children it is impossible to obtain any sort of history from the child, and the doctor has to obtain what history he can from relatives, social workers, police officers, and sometimes from other children. In such situations the doctor must remember that the accounts given to him are rarely accurate and are often grossly inaccurate (p 90).

There are often pressures which can detract from a doctor's objectivity: 'a crying child; angry or anguished relatives and law enforcement officers or social workers who have already made up their minds and look to the physician only to confirm their beliefs' (p 86).

A preconception that abuse has taken place can affect an interview in a number of ways. First, the child denies abuse, the interviewer may continue to press on with the questioning in the belief that the child is blocking the fact of abuse. Such an approach is consistent with the theory of 'pressure' interviews which has been described in these terms: 'it is necessary to match the trauma which the child has suffered through the abuse by placing equal pressure on the child to talk about what has happened'.[5]

If, in fact, the child has not been abused then two dangers are apparent. First, the child may be persuaded to say something that is not true. Second, there is the danger that the child may be disturbed by the interview.

It is now clear that many interviews during the Cleveland Affair suffered from these very faults. The Cleveland Inquiry Report noted that:

> There was a presumption that abuse had occurred and the child was either not disclosing or denying . . . and those conducting the interviews seemed unaware of the extent of pressure even coercion in their approach. (Cleveland Inquiry Report, para 12.42[1])

Such coercion might include repetitions or variations of a question in order to outflank a denial.

Preconceptions that abuse has taken place will also affect the form of questions used. Leading questions are an undesirable example. It is equally undesirable to prompt a young child by using the dolls in a suggestive or leading manner. Multiple-choice questions can also be counter-productive and were criticised in evidence in *Re N*: 'In the face of two choice questions, the incriminating choice was always second and a child, not thinking very clearly would choose the most recent suggestion'. (Dr Connell, *Re N* [1987] 1 FLR 280, at p 287f)

Hypothetical questions are also undesirable. These tend to be employed where a child has denied abuse throughout the interview. A change of track is then adopted 'If Daddy touched you where did he touch you?' There is a superficial attraction in using such a question in these circumstances. It is, however, a dishonest approach and it is also potentially confusing to a child who might think 'is this a game?'

There is then the loaded question. This at least has not been elevated to the status of a tactic. It occasionally surfaces where the interviewer is inexperienced and/or believes that abuse has taken place and misses a logical step in the interview process. It is a variety of the 'when did you stop beating your wife' type of question which can be confusing for even an adult witness.

Inducements

In one fairly recent case the interviewer responded to any answer which indicated abuse with the words 'Good boy! Good boy!' Any answer denying abuse was ignored.

This approach can be justified on the ground that the child may be reluctant or fearful of disclosing abuse and may need re-assurance. However, the dangers of such an approach are obvious in the context of a fairly long interview in which a single question is repeated, perhaps in a variety of forms. Even a young child will quickly pick up what answers will please his interviewer and which will not. Before passing on from this subject, let it be noted in one such interview the inducements came in the form of boiled sweets!

Discussions of allegations in front of the child prior to interview

This ought never to happen since it undermines the quality of any disclosures that may be made. We are looking for spontaneity of complaint in the child's own words or gestures. Anything which detracts from this will affect the evidential weight attached to the interview.

Abuse or no abuse?

A much criticised feature of the conduct of these interviews has been the failure of interviewers to seek out and identify indications that the child has not been abused.

Unqualified interviewers

Many of the practices described above are the result of these dolls being used by individuals who are quite unqualified to use them. In too many cases to number, the dolls have been produced like so many puppets. There are no legal controls restricting the use of these dolls.

The use of anatomically correct dolls by unqualified individuals was criticised in the Cleveland Inquiry Report in strong terms (see chapter 12, paragraphs 55 to 64 inclusive[1]).

Lawyers and clinicians

If abuse by a parent is diagnosed in an interview and denied by the alleged perpetrator, then of course, the clinician's findings will be subject to the closest scrutiny. A false or erroneous allegation of abuse against a parent opens up horrifying possibilities; the children taken into care; the loss of a spouse; possible criminal charges and the prospects of being shunned by all and sundry.

Regrettably, in some cases where abuse is diagnosed one encounters doctors, social workers and child psychiatrists apparently over ready to support each others views. Into the arena comes the parents' lawyers, partisan and hostile, asking awkward questions and challenging commonly held assumptions.

Such a lawyer is in part a product of our adversarial system of justice. A system which co-exists uneasily with Wardship and Care jurisdictions which are constituted for the purpose of protecting the child and which are theoretically non-adversarial.

Hostility is particularly marked in cases where the evidence of abuse stems largely or wholly from diagnostic interviews conducted with the aid of anatomically correct dolls. In the search for reliability the courts have been refining methods of obtaining evidence for centuries. Consequently, certain forms of questions and methods of eliciting evidence are not generally permitted because it is recognised that the answers given will be unreliable. An answer obtained by a leading question is one example. Not surprisingly some lawyers exhibit a degree of professional outrage over diagnostic interviews which may, and sometimes do, flout every convention governing the eliciting of evidence.

Cross examination of clinicians tends, therefore, to be lengthy and hostile. It is nonetheless the best aid to an assessment of the evidence. It identifies issues, tests expertise and in this context it provides vital motivation for clinicians to constantly re-evaluate and modify techniques.

There are also some unfortunate consequences:

> Certain psychiatrists in practice are so repelled at the prospect of having their work attacked in this way in court, and so concerned about possible negative publicity following the cases that they are not prepared to see such children for assessment.[6]

The hostility of lawyers has been matched only by the vigour with which these interview techniques have been defended by the clinicians. Both professional bodies have strong claims to expertise in this field.

The struggle for control over the form of interviews or individual questions is well illustrated by section 32 of the Criminal Justice Act 1988 which provides for children under 14 to give evidence in criminal trials via a live video link. The passage of the Act was preceded by a bitter debate as to whether questioning should be carried out by counsel or some third party, a therapist, perhaps. That battle was resolved in favour of the lawyers, for now. Though the adherents of the opposite point of view were numerous and vocal.

Both lawyers and clinicians will have to give a little ground. The nature of the work demands that clinicians have some latitude in the way these diagnostic interviews are conducted. The quid pro quo is that all such interviews are videotaped. In the words of Latey J in *Re M* [1987] 1 FLR 293G, 'this is the minimum requirement to meet the interests not only of justice between the parties but also of the court doing its best to arrive at the truth'.

References

1. *Report of the Inquiry into Child Abuse in Cleveland.* Cm 412, HMSO, 1988.
2. The Editors of *Family Law Reports* have compiled a number of cases in which the use of anatomically correct dolls is discussed and analysed. These are set out at [1987] 1 FLR 269–346.
3. Bentovim, A, Tranter, M, and Vizard, E (1987). Interviewing sexually abused children, *Adoption and Fostering*, Feb, p 20.
4. Paul, D Whatever happened to baby Jane? *Medicine, Science and Law*, 26, Number 2.
5. Douglas, G, and Wilmore, C (1987). Diagnostic interviews as evidence in cases of child sexual abuse. *Family Law*, 17, 151.
6. Vizard, E (1987). *Family Law*, 17 at p 32.

CHAPTER 8

The Role of the Official Solicitor in Child Abuse Cases

MICHAEL HINCHLIFFE

Solicitor

I spent many days in the Autumn of 1987 at the Cleveland Child Abuse Inquiry in Middlesbrough listening to evidence. I read the reports prepared by members of the Official Solicitor's staff of interviews with children and others in Cleveland. My overwhelming impression was of children who were bewildered by events and often unconcerned with the activities of the experts. I was reminded of the great responsibility which is thus placed upon child care professionals in all fields. I will say more about Cleveland later on. The Inquiry required a huge commitment of time and expertise for the Department in the field of child abuse, and especially child sexual abuse. It was sadly already a very familiar area for us.

The Official Solicitor in children's cases

In 1987, the Official Solicitor accepted appointment as guardian ad litem or next friend in approximately 850 children's cases. At the present time, his overall case load of children's cases totals approximately 2200. The representation of children who are the subject of wardship, divorce (custody) and High Court adoption proceedings forms a substantial proportion of the Official Solicitor's work.

There are approximately 140 full-time civil servants working in the Official Solicitor's Office. Engaged wholly or partly in handling children's cases are 39 members of staff, including the Official Solicitor himself, Mr David Venables, and his Deputy. His staff are organised in five divisions each overseen by a Senior Executive Officer. The bulk of the case work is handled by the Higher Executive Officers and Executive Officers in each division. Apart from the Official Solicitor and Deputy Official Solicitor, there are two other qualified Solicitors working in this field, of whom I am one.

In children's cases the Official Solicitor may represent a mentally disordered or minor parent. In the vast majority of cases he acts for the child himself or herself. When representing a child, the

Official Solicitor almost always acts as Solicitor as well as guardian ad litem.

A typical case

A typical wardship case would begin with the court file being sent to the Official Solicitor's office. Although the bulk of the work on a particular case would normally be handled by an individual Officer, each case will be reviewed by the Divisional Officer on a regular basis and referred where necessary to the Official Solicitor himself or one of the other lawyers. In addition, there is a deliberate pooling of knowledge of individual cases to ensure continuity of representation should the primary case worker have to relinquish the case for any reason. The work is essentially a corporate effort.

Having read the court file, the Officer will interview all individuals (quite apart from the strict parties to the proceedings) who may have a view that is relevant to the child's welfare. Advice will be given on the joinder of third parties as appropriate. The evidence is reviewed and where necessary supplemented by the Official Solicitor's own expert evidence. In child abuse cases it is increasingly common for the Official Solicitor to instruct a child psychiatrist or other medical expert who may in particularly difficult cases spend many hours interviewing the child and other individuals involved.

The Official Solicitor will ensure, so far as it lies within his power to do so, that affidavits are filed promptly and that the hearings of children's cases in which he is involved are not subject to unwarranted delay. Because the Official Solicitor does not apply for legal aid in children's cases, work on a case can be started immediately he accepts the appointment as the child's guardian ad litem.

Although prepared by the individual case worker, the Official Solicitor's report is always reviewed and signed by the Official Solicitor himself or his Deputy.

The hearing

The Official Solicitor briefs counsel and (through his representative) attends the main hearing with counsel. He is thus able on behalf of the child to cross-examine witnesses as well as tendering his own witnesses and making submissions. Should circumstances warrant it, if for instance the Official Solicitor has not had time to prepare a formal report, then his representative will be prepared to undergo cross-examination.

Specific tasks may be imposed upon the Official Solicitor by the court either before or after the main hearing, for instance the determination of details of access ordered by the court. Because of the continuing nature of the wardship jurisdiction, it is by no means uncommon for a particular case to remain live in the Official Solicitor's office for up to ten years or more. There will be periodic referrals to court, sometimes at very short notice. One of the family lawyers on the Official Solicitor's staff is always available to deal with any complicated or urgent matters which may require his attention, including applications to the court. The Official Solicitor will also deal with any other proceedings or legal problems with which the child may become involved (other than criminal proceedings), and if appropriate he will institute proceedings on behalf of the child. As well as the more obvious matters such as personal injury claims, the Official Solicitor may make application on behalf of the child for compensation in respect of injuries arising from a crime to the Criminal Injuries Compensation Board. If necessary the Official Solicitor will administer the award for the child until his minority. This is an area which has in the past often been overlooked. I suspect that it has not up to now been widely appreciated that the Scheme extends to crimes other than crimes of violence, such as child sexual abuse.

The Official Solicitor can offer some assistance in criminal matters. It may for instance be desired to call a child as a witness in criminal proceedings. Although the Official Solicitor does not normally represent children in criminal proceedings, his Officers have occasionally made application for a witness summons in respect of a child to be set aside,

The voice of the child

The Official Solicitor sees his primary function as being to give the child a voice in the proceedings. The child is almost always seen by his representative, whatever his age. The Official Solicitor's submissions are based on his assessment of the best interests of the child, having due regard to the child's wishes according to his age and level of understanding.

It must be acknowledged that there may be occasions when the views of the child are so fundamentally inconsistent with what the Official Solicitor perceives to be in the child's best interests that the Official Solicitor feels obliged to make an alternative submission to the court. An example is the drug-addicted 17-year-old girl who wishes to continue an association with a man who supplies her with drugs. The views of the child will of course still be presented in the Official Solicitor's report and the child at the hearing will be given an opportunity to present his or her views to the Judge in private.

The Official Solicitor's Officers interviewed many children during the Cleveland Inquiry. One of my lasting impressions of Cleveland will be the many accounts, often extremely harrowing, of sexual abuse at the hands of often trusted adults and the frequently expressed gratitude and relief at the intervention of the medical experts and Social Services in Cleveland. On the one hand many feel the public still do not fully appreciate the extent of the incidence of child sexual abuse in our society. On the other hand, there are those who argue that such is the range of activities which may be labelled child sexual abuse that there is a danger of over-reaction in less serious cases.

Cleveland Inquiry

None of the children in Cleveland who spoke to the Official Solicitor's Officers complained of being examined by doctors without consent. It has become accepted practice for doctors to look for consent from the child himself, when able to understand the issues involved, at least since the House of Lord's decision in *Gillick v West Norfolk Area Health Authority* [1986] AC 112. The difficulty is that very often children suspected of being victims of abuse are too young to give a reasoned consent to examination or treatment. In practice, there is little a very young child can do but go along with any proposed examination and therefore this does place a heavy responsibility upon the doctor, particularly where it may not be appropriate to consult the parents if they are the suspected abusers.

A logical extension of the issue of consent is the child's power to control information generated during an investigation. It is a widely held view that no child should ever be compelled to give evidence in court in any proceedings relating to alleged sexual, or indeed physical abuse, of that child. Even with innovations such as video links for giving evidence in court, the whole process is bound to remain harrowing for many children. The Official Solicitor in his submissions to the Cleveland Inquiry stated that although those conducting investigations may legitimately seek to persuade a child to talk about abuse as an unburdening process, this must be kept distinct from so-called 'disclosure work' as a means of gathering material for use in court. If the child cannot or will not talk, then the matter ought to rest there, at any rate until the child himself decides that he is able to talk. This approach, by promoting the best interests of the child in the widest sense rather than the establishment of the truth of the allegations, may render more difficult the management of the case by the Social Services. Given the frequent absence of physical evidence of sexual abuse, and the difficulty of establishing for certain that there has been no abuse, the outcome of some investigations is bound to be inconclusive.

Dealing with the abuser

This is a controversial area. Some of the older children in particular who spoke to the Official Solicitor's Officers in Cleveland complained of a lack of vigour on the part of the police following-up their cases and prosecuting the offenders. On the other hand, many people argue that an admission by the offender, which will greatly facilitate the investigation, is less likely to be forthcoming if the probable consequence is prosecution, conviction and sentence. The child will often be well aware of the dilemma. Should he tell the police that he has been abused by his father and risk the break-up of the family, with the father going to prison and the child himself going to a foster home or a Children's Home? There is not space for me here to discuss the various responses which the criminal law might have to a convicted abuser. The victims must be protected. But there are those who argue for tough therapy programmes rather than long prison sentences, for some offenders. There may be a conflict between punishment of sexual offenders and the effect this has on the child victim where continuing contact with the offender is still desired by and may still be a benefit to the child. The Courts have already indicated that the fact that a father has seriously sexually abused his child will not necessarily rule out any access: *H v H* (1988) *The Times*, 4 October, Court of Appeal.

The first response

Where a suspicion of child sexual abuse has first arisen, the authorities must consider the safety of the child. During the crisis period in Cleveland applications to Magistrates for Place of Safety Orders appear to have been the routine first response. The contention was that immediate separation from the perpetrator was necessary in order to spare the child further pressure not to speak of what had occurred. The danger is that an early application for a Place of Safety Order may cause polarisation of attitudes between

Social Services and the family. Many now feel the immediate protection of the child is best secured by negotiation with the family where possible. There is wide support for the proposals for an 'Emergency Protection Order' in the Children Bill now before Paliament. Emphasis on the emergency nature of the provision, the explicit definition of the powers and responsibilities of the applicant in respect of the child, and the presumption in favour of access for the parents are key elements of the proposals which are designed to overcome many of the difficulties experienced in Cleveland.

It has been decided not to proceed with the Office of Child Protection which was first proposed in the Cleveland Inquiry Report (see Appendix II) and which was the subject of a consultation paper issued by the Lord Chancellor's Department in July 1988. The consultation paper also proposed that there should be arrangements for different child care cases more easily to find their way to the appropriate level in the court system. There are provisions to this effect in the new Bill.

When is a guardian ad litem needed?

Even in cases of child sexual abuse it should not be a matter of routine for a guardian ad litem to be appointed to represent the child in wardship proceedings. The governing principle was most recently re-stated by Mr Justice Sheldon in *Re A, B, C and D* [1988] 2 FLR 500:

> In general—and apart from cases involving an older child who has and is old enough to express an informed view as to his or to her future—such a course should be adopted only in difficult cases and where the intervention of a Guardian ad litem is likely to be of particular assistance to the Court. It is not a sufficient reason in itself that the other parties to the proceedings ask for or consent to such a step—and in many cases, as where all that is required is some independent report on one or more matters in issue, it may well be sufficient for such a report to be ordered from one of the Court Welfare Officers.

On the other hand, where for instance a psychiatric report on the child is needed, it will usually be preferable for a guardian ad litem to instruct the psychiatrist to ensure that he is fully briefed and that the other parties and experts in the case are able to be cross-examined by counsel instructed by the guardian ad litem on behalf of the child where appropriate.

The courts have made it clear that in wardship proceedings the Official Solicitor is to be the first person to be invited to act as guardian ad litem of the child. While it may be desirable for the guardian ad litem from earlier juvenile court proceedings to continue to act in that capacity within the wardship, there are a number of factors which should be borne in mind by guardians ad litem. The Official Solicitor referred to this in his submissions to the Cleveland Inquiry. Apart from the Official Solicitor's particular expertise in wardship matters, there is the importance of continuity of representation, to which I have referred above.

I have recently had experience of an adoption matter in which a panel guardian ad litem successfully sought leave to institute wardship proceedings, thereby taking the adoption proceedings into the High Court. The Official Solicitor was asked by the court to act as the child's guardian ad litem in the adoption proceedings in the High Court. Naturally it was pointed out to the court that the existing guardian ad litem might wish to remain in the case. It was only after months of confusion that his solicitor wrote to say that he had moved to another part of the country and 'largely ceased working as a guardian ad litem'.

The Official Solicitor's costs

The Official Solicitor does not as a matter of policy apply for legal aid to cover his costs in wardship proceedings. Applications are made in other circumstances and there is no difficulty in this for the Official Solicitor in that he acts as guardian ad litem and solicitor rolled into one. In wardship and adoption proceedings, however, it is the Official Solicitor's practice to seek for at least a proportion of his costs to be met by the local authority involved. In order to avoid protracted arguments in individual cases, agreements have been reached with a number of local authorities fixing a percentage of the Official Solicitor's costs which will be met by the local authority in each of its cases which involves the Official Solicitor. If necessary, for instance, in cases where there is no local authority involved and all parties are legally aided, the Official Solicitor will not look to any other party for his costs, which will fall to be met from central government funds.

Contacting the Official Solicitor

The Official Solicitor's Office is at:
Penderel House, 287, High Holborn, London WC1V 7HP.

I and other members of his staff are always available to try to assist with queries and discuss cases in which his involvement may be necessary. The telephone number is 01-936 7127/6000.

It is worth emphasising, I think, that the Official Solicitor covers the whole of England and Wales and his Officers conduct interviews and cover hearings wherever and whenever necessary.

CHAPTER 9

The Juvenile Court: Forum for Child Abuse Proceedings

JOHN ELLISON
Solicitor

The context

Twelve formative years as a child care solicitor for a local authority have made me acutely aware of the problems and uncertainties for local authorities and the courts in care proceedings based on child abuse. Nowhere are these problems and uncertainties more evident than in the Juvenile Court arena. Here I mention and illustrate some of them against a backcloth of the legislation and its application in recent judicial decisions.

A high proportion of care proceedings continue to be conducted in the Juvenile Court under section 1 of the Children and Young Persons Act 1969. Most are brought by local authorities; the rest by the Police or the NSPCC.

In the early years of the 1969 Act social services departments of local authorities hardly ever resorted to the wardship jurisdiction of the High Court to protect children and decide their future. Some authorities still find themselves in the High Court only rarely. But many now rely on wardship proceedings where cases do not seem to fit the grounds for proceedings laid out in section 1 of the 1969 Act or where wardship seems for some other reason to be appropriate. Other reasons might be the unusual complexity of the case, the need for some order (such as an injunction) unavailable in the Juvenile Court, or the existence of international factors, such as the earlier abduction of the child abroad.

Juvenile Court care proceedings are split into two stages. First, the 'primary condition' defined in section 1 must be proved, normally on oral evidence. Second, once the 'primary condition' is established, the court considers 'disposal' with the help of reports and spoken submissions. A key report is independently prepared by a guardian ad litem appointed by the court to act in the child's interests. The guardian ad litem may be a social worker from another local authority or a 'freelance' guardian. The 'disposal' options are, in most cases, a care or supervision order. A care order enables the local authority to place the child with a parent, with some other relative, in a children's home, with a foster parent or even with prospective adopters without natural family access. A supervision order is a directive for monitoring of the child's progress while placed (usually) with a parent.

Care proceedings abound with difficulties in all courts, but in the Juvenile Court are augmented by a bizarre combination of 'rough and tumble' practices and a tradition of pedantically framed legislation more suited to the court's criminal jurisdiction. However, improvements were recommended by the DHSS in 1985[1] and by the subsequent White Paper published in 1987.[2] The Children Bill is now going through Parliament. It will be some time before it is implemented.

Whether proceedings are justified or not, they give rise to tensions, anxieties and anger for parents, and distress and confusion for children. For social workers to think and plan with professional objectivity in such an emotive context is not easy.

The decision to start proceedings: problems and implications

The statutory requirement for children of 5 or over to be present at the Juvenile Court at the first hearing of care proceedings, and their frequent presence at later hearings, inevitably tends to heighten the emotional atmosphere in and outside court. In some cases great efforts are made to keep children, anxious not to be confronted with their parents, out of sight but near to hand for brief production to the Bench. In other cases children meet their parents outside court, not always with happy results. I recall one case where a teenage boy hid, with extreme embarrassment, from his mentally ill mother under a table in the waiting area.

To decide upon care proceedings, whether emergency removal commences the process or not, is a very serious and often a very difficult decision for social services departments. Thereafter to carry out investigations and assessment and to resolve on a final approach to the proceedings and the child's future is equally problematic. On the one hand well-tried practices need to be followed. On the other hand inflexibility needs to be avoided. Each case presents different challenges. Imagination and the willingness to take risks, though not any risk, seem to be essential features of the exercise.

The process of investigation and assessment on a continuous basis has obvious legal implications in the context of care proceedings. Interviews with parents, children and others are intended not only to be fed into the decision-making process of the social services department, but to provide information for the court. Social workers may need guidance as to whether the investigation process has been sufficient for this purpose, whether reporting the interviews will be excluded by the rules of evidence and so on.

In some cases a social services investigation is fraught with difficulty. How should, for example, a social services department respond to being informed of an ancient allegation in respect of a child still of tender years? In a case reported in 1987 a High Court judge endorsed the view of a psychiatrist that to investigate a remark made by a child two years previously (when 2 years old), when the family was still together, was a 'grave disruption and a mistake'.[3]

In the case of Kimberley Carlile, on the other hand, the Inquiry Report (published in 1987) on her death criticised a senior social worker for not pursuing a medical examination on this 4-year-old child or contact with her despite obvious reasons for concern. Child care legal advisers can give useful assistance in relation to such issues.

The child care legal adviser, it may be said, has a different function from legal advisers in some other fields. Advice is not aimed at 'firming up' cases, at accumulating evidence *for* a case, but at learning more of the facts and factual background. The information gained will then have the effect either of reducing or increasing concerns and the need for proceedings. Cases 'firm up' or weaken as more information emerges. The duty of child care legal rep resentatives to ensure that all the relevant evidence, for and against the authority's case, is brought to the attention of other parties and the court, is accepted by many practitioners.

The child care legal adviser also has the function of monitoring social work practice against legislative requirements. This need has recently been underlined by the failure of Cleveland County Council, identified in the Cleveland Inquiry Report, to supply solicitor representatives at more than 3 out of 175 case conferences between April and June 1987. This failure may have facilitated decisions and the continuation of practices which were out of step with legislation relating to emergency court orders.

The formal grounds for proceedings

The legal adviser, in any particular Juvenile Court case, also has to consider whether the facts add up to a case within section 1 of the 1969 Act.

This is not always obvious, especially at the outset, if the process has been begun by an emergency. Most Juvenile Court child abuse cases are brought on the 'proper development ground' set out in section 1(2)(a) of the Act. The technical allegation is that the child's 'proper development is being avoidably impaired or neglected, or his health is being avoidably impaired or neglected or he is being ill-treated'.

This includes and excludes a multitude of sins. There are 'battering' cases, which might be treated as including injuries caused by striking with the hand or with an implement, brain injuries caused to young children by shaking, bone fractures due to the violent twisting of an arm or leg, sexual assault and injuries caused by the application of heat through, perhaps, scalding or touching with a lighted cigarette end. Here the 'ill-treatment' part of the formal allegation is of particular relevance.

Then there are 'neglect' cases. Neglect cases may involve a 'dirty house' element, a failure to feed a baby or to provide food for an older child, a failure to ensure a tolerable level of hygiene, or to facilitate medical treatment. Neglect cases may also be founded by a failure to ensure physical safety, for example, not preventing a young child's fall from a flat window despite earlier warnings of the danger or, conceivably, relying on the family's watch dog as a babysitter. Neglect is neglect of 'proper development' or 'health', so a child who (through avoidable neglect) fails to thrive physically, intellectually or emotionally, or a child who is encouraged not to go to school, will fall into this pigeon-hole.

There are, of course, many occasions where a 'proper development' case is a clear one. For example, where a 10-year-old girl had repeated urinary infections and persistent medical advice as to the need for tests and treatment (having regard to risk of future kidney damage) had been ignored by the parent, it was obvious that the child's health was being neglected.

The 'proper development' argument becomes more difficult to sustain where the causes of injuries or a failure to thrive are uncertain or subject to professional disagreement.

Suppose a case where a baby a few months old receives bruises in the temple area. Bruises on the head naturally awaken more medical concern than bruises to the limbs. The father's explanation is that, while carrying the baby down some unstable steps he fell with the baby, landing on top of the baby. Suppose, again, that one doctor, a junior doctor, finds the parental explanation quite inadequate while a paediatrician, asked for a second opinion, finds the explanation entirely plausible. Seniority will not, of course, be a factor of great importance in itself in determining the value of evidence.

The court will have to decide which medical view to prefer. If it prefers the junior doctor's view, the court may then infer, taking into account the other evidence, that the child was ill-treated or neglected. If the court does not prefer the junior doctor's view, the 'proper development' case would seem to fall to the ground.

The advocate for the local authority may be a solicitor experienced in child care proceedings. But often solicitors with slight experience of child care law and the practice assumptions of social workers are at court to present the case. And again, some local authorities rely on court officers as their advocates: often ex-social workers or ex-police officers, who may develop much experience without a firm basis in legal training or qualifications.

Whatever the advocate's qualifications, aptitude and experience, questions arising in the case I have just described may benefit from legal comment. Faced with an instructing social services department which has serious concerns about the welfare of the baby whose temple area was bruised in such doubtful circumstances, should Juvenile Court proceedings be encouraged or discouraged? If the child has been removed from home, should the child now be returned in the light of the medical disagreement? Should the proceedings, if begun, be gracefully withdrawn? The local authority lawyer's role in assisting the social workers concerned with the child to make a decision may be of importance.

A suggested approach might be, in general terms, first to clarify whether both doctors have considered the same questions on the basis of the same material. It might then be advisable to be sure of the reasons of each for their conclusions. If, each being aware of the other's position, the two doctors retain their views unmodified, if the junior doctor's reasons for scepticism seem to have weight, and if social workers accordingly (and perhaps for other reasons too) conclude the child to be likely to be at unacceptable risk, then Juvenile Court proceedings would seem to have some basis in law. A position could be taken up as to whether or not the child, if already removed under an emergency order, should be returned home and as to what future orders should be sought and what further action taken.

In the Juvenile Court the 1969 Act provides that it is not enough for the institutor of proceedings to prove the 'proper development' condition. It must also be proved that the child 'is in need of care or control which he is unlikely to receive unless the court makes an order . . .' All this is in section 1(2).

Guidance as to what the Bench must take into account in applying this test was given by Lord Justice Butler-Sloss when a High Court judge in *M v Westminster City Council*, reported in 1985.[4] She said: 'It seems clear to me that one must, in considering a care or control condition, look at all the circumstances including the future and, indeed, including other aspects of the past.'

It is probably fair to comment that if the 'proper development' aspect of a care proceedings case is found, the need for 'care and control' is likely in most circumstances to flow naturally out of it especially if, for example, voluntary social work with the family has failed to secure the child's well-being. So I return to the problem of proving the 'proper development' condition.

Sometimes the core of the case is parental drinking. The drinking problem may have continued for years, but the effect on the child, despite inquiries, may be open to speculation. To what extent was the child neglected or otherwise placed at risk? Was the child left unattended for long periods? Was there a risk of accidental fire, for example? Had any such accidents happened?

The answers may be unclear and even where there are some definite answers, the inferences to be drawn may not be easy. Suppose two recent incidents of definite neglect during drinking are uncovered. Can it then be reasonably inferred, especially if there has been admitted or proved drinking on other occasions when the parent has had the child's care, that neglect is likely to have occurred on those other occasions as well?

Then there may be observable effects on the child. He or she may be haunted by fears of fires, having had in the past one or more experiences of fires started. He or she may be burdened, at a tender age, with responsibility for the family's safety. A nightly self-appointed task may be to stay awake until the parent has fallen

asleep in an armchair, ensuring that the last cigarette is exting-
uished and not dropped and left to smoulder on a carpet. He or
she may have been neglected in other ways, for example by having
extreme and long untreated dental decay. All such factors add to
the 'proper development' ground and also go to lend force to the
second argument: that the child is 'in need of care of control'.

It is conceivable, in a case of the sort here described, that at the
effective hearing the institutor of proceedings may fail to convince
the court that the 'proper development' condition applies or, if
it does, that the care and control test is also met. This could occur
even though the facts are not in dispute. The reason could be that
since the occasion which gave rise to the proceedings, three or
four months or longer may have passed, and circumstances may
have, or may seem to have, changed. The child may have been
in care, first under a Place of Safety Order and then under interim
orders, and may have received the required medical or dental treatment. The parents, upset by the child's removal and the proceedings, and relieved of the child's care, may have made a major effort
to deal with the drinking problem. By the time the effective hearing
takes place, the progress of access contact and evidence of a suspen-
sion of drinking may persuade the court to find the case not proved.

It is arguable, however, that the dismissal of proceedings on the
facts given may be difficult to reconcile with the broad interpretation of the 'proper development' condition approved in the judgement of Lord Brandon in Re D [1987][5] considered later in this
chapter.

The order sought by the local authority will, usually, be a care
or supervision order. If circumstances have improved in respect
of a child removed into care, the social workers may well favour
the child's return home, and if the return home is accomplished
before the proceedings are completed, may favour a supervision
order. They may even go further and recommend withdrawal of
the proceedings altogether with, perhaps, the prospect instead of
voluntary social work contact with the family.

The evidence of abuse—accepting that the term 'abuse' is crude and unilluminating—may sometimes consist of little more than the child's own actions, statements and wishes. Take the example of a 14-year-old girl who swallows an overdose of tablets and who then, admitted to hospital, states that she does not wish to return home, making allegations of a sexual nature against a parent and giving these as the main reason for not wishing to return. If her wishes and allegations are persisted in, and are accepted by the professionals involved, it is likely, in practice, I suggest, even faced with steady parental denial of allegations, that the court will find her 'proper development' has been neglected and 'care and control' tests satisfied, whether the girl herself gives evidence or not.

At the same time there are cases where an element of the child's wish to leave home (and possibly a motive for allegations of physical abuse) seems to be the desire for a freer life than permitted at home. In such circumstances the social services department bringing the proceedings needs to satisfy itself that there is sufficient reason for protective action on the basis of the 'proper development' (or another) ground. If it is so satisfied the court will consider the issue itself at a later stage, and the child's own wishes and statements may not be necessarily accepted by the court.

It should be said, perhaps, that to find a case not proved in respect of a teenager who is reluctant to return home may risk a further breach between the child and parent, and may conceivably add to the damage in relationships. The child may also be placed at physical risk. I am aware of one, not recent, case where, I gather, after the failure of care proceedings on appeal, the parent sought promptly, on his son's return home, to confine and assault him. The son succeeded in escaping through a window. A Place of Safety Order and fresh proceedings, this time successful, followed.

In cases where two parents or two parent-figures are caring for a child, it may be that one parent may be associated with the neglect or ill-treatment, while the other is not. Again, even where there is only one parent 'on the scene', the problems which justify the proceedings may be associated with a relative or friend. In such cases there may sometimes be arguably insufficient evidence of parental neglect to prove the 'proper development' condition, or, even if there is sufficient evidence for this purpose, there may not be sufficient to prove the 'care or control' condition.

Let us imagine another hypothetical situation, an amalgam of cases met with in practice. A young mother, who has had housing and other difficulties, cares for her 2-year-old son satisfactorily, though at times loses patience with him. His development is normal. She meets a young man who moves into the home. He is violent to both mother and child and ill-treats the child over a period of weeks. The mother is frightened he will leave her and frightened of reporting the ill-treatment of her son. The ill-treatment leads to the child suffering a broken arm as a result of being violently seized and held by the mother's cohabitee. The grandmother reports her concern to a social worker and the social worker finds the child at home injured and in need of treatment.

In this case the 'proper development' condition, because of the ill-treatment, will be clear unless an accident (the accident not being due to neglect) can be offered as the explanation for the injury. The 'care or control' test may be established by reference to the fact (among other circumstances) that the mother was not herself able to protect the child. She did not evict her cohabitee or leave the premises herself with the child or even promptly report the injury to a doctor.

It is quite clear that the 'proper development' ground for Juvenile Court care proceedings must be based on damage caused to, or neglect or ill-treatment suffered by, the child. For the child to be 'at risk' is not enough, even if the risk of future harm is high and unacceptable. Thus in cases where, for example, a baby is born to a mentally ill single parent mother whose proximity to the child is thought to be an unacceptable danger, unless the mother has been given sufficient opportunity to care for, and neglect, the child to substantiate a case in the Juvenile Court, it would seem that if proceedings are essential wardship would be the desirable means of protecting the child.

Again, where a person believed to have committed actions amounting to sexual or other physical abuse of a young child previously, but not convicted of such an offence, becomes a carer or part carer of a young child, it may not be possible to mount a satisfactory case in the Juvenile Court. If evidence can be called to support the allegation against this person in respect of the other child, the 'standard of proof' should, it appears, as a result of a case reported in 1987,[6] be stricter than the normal 'balance of probabilities' standard of proof. But if this hurdle were successfully crossed, it is conceivable that the local authority could argue the present child's development is being 'neglected' by being cared for by such an unsuitable person.

This would be an unusual (though perhaps a reasonable) argument for the Juvenile Court. The authority might in practice be faced by the argument that whether or not the allegation is true, the primary carer of the child is well able to ensure the child is protected. The authority, on such thin ice, as a result of the present technical requirements for the child in the proceedings to have faced more than risk, might again opt for wardship proceedings if proceedings seem necessary.

As I have said, the general principle in 'proper development' proceedings in the 1969 Act is that the child must have been harmed or neglected. It is not normally enough for the child to be 'at risk', yet in section 1 of the Act there are also two 'risk' grounds for proceedings. These are, however, drawn so narrowly and particularly that they are only occasionally available to be relied on. They cover the situation where a person with a conviction for a child abuse offence (a 'Schedule I offence') has joined or may join a household of the child to be protected, and, second, the situation where a case on the 'proper development' ground has already been proved in respect of another child of the household. I leave the exact boundaries of these two 'risk' grounds for proceedings to larger and more detailed investigations.

Sometimes it may occur, with older children, that a case of alleged 'abuse' is linked with a conspicuous problem of control of the child. In such a case it is possible that proceedings may be both on the 'proper development' and on the 'beyond control' ground (section 1(2)(d)). Suppose, for example, that the mother of a 10 or 11-year-old boy, finding him to have wet his bed, becomes angry and strikes him, causing a bruise. To add to the picture, suppose his mother has, in the absence of a male partner, habitually accorded her son the status of 'the man of the house'. The boy, unaccustomed much of the time to being treated as a child, retaliates by biting his mother and then runs out of the house, going to the police station and refusing to return. His 'proper development' may have been neglected by inconsistent treatment, and the single act of physical ill-treatment of the child may be of an insubstantial nature, taken in isolation. The breach between child and parent may disappear with a reconciliation. Such a case raises a question, in some cases commenced, as to the possibility of withdrawal. The arguments for particular solutions are often finely balanced.

In recent years decided cases have had the effect of encouraging a broad interpretation of what has to be proved to sustain a Juvenile Court care proceedings case. This has been valuable guidance for the courts and welcome to those acting for children and local authorities.

Perhaps the two most important of these cases (both mentioned above) are *M v Westminster City Council* [1985],[4] a Divisional Court case, and *Re D* [1987],[5] a House of Lords decision.

In *M v Westminster City Council*, an appeal from a decision of the Westminster North Juvenile Court 'by way of case stated', judicial attention was concentrated upon the meaning of the requirement that the child's proper development 'is being' avoidably impaired or neglected. In many care proceedings at the date of the effective hearing there may not be current evidence of a failure of proper development or ill-treatment. The child may be in care or may have been returned home following the incident provoking the proceedings without further adverse evidence of inadequate care. Despite an attempt to persuade the court that 'is' must mean 'now', that is, 'this minute' or 'this day', the Divisional Court insisted on a broader approach.

The case concerned twin girls of just over a year. The proceedings had been based on the mother's drinking, the father's violence and abuse to the mother, her reluctance to separate from him, their leaving the children unattended and not responding to the children's needs at times of stress.

Mrs Justice Butler-Sloss (as she then was) stated, after rejecting the argument that the child's development must be avoidably prevented at the time of the hearing:

> A child's development is a continuing process. The present must be relevant in the context of what has happened in the past and it becomes a matter of degree as to how far in the past you go . . . . Therefore, the magistrates approach to this case, whereby they said that you look at the position when the proceedings were started and are entitled to interpret it in the light of anything which has happened since, was an entirely proper way for them to consider this matter . . .

Applying this approach to the case of these two little twin girls she went on to say:

> the fact that the children had been left alone, their presence during violence, the evidence of a drink and the parents' lack of reaction to children at times of stress, led the justices to the inevitable conclusion that their proper development was avoidably being prevented or neglected.

Re D, the House of Lords case, dealt with an uncommon, but not unique, justification for protective action: the birth of a child suffering from symptoms of withdrawal from drugs. The mother had persistently taken drugs during pregnancy in excess of medical prescription although aware of the potential damage to her unborn child.

The Reading Juvenile Court heard the case when the child was approaching 5 months. Proceedings had begun with a Place of Safety Order a few weeks after the child's birth and had been followed by a series of interim care orders. Neither parent had had the care of the child since the birth.

The Juvenile Court, considering the grounds for the 'proper development' condition, found it satisfied. An appeal by way of case stated then proceeded through several judicial levels: the Divisional Court, the Court of Appeal and then the House of Lords. The two highest appeal courts both found the Juvenile Court to have been right, on the basis of the approach approved in *M v Westminster City Council*.

In *Re D* Lord Brandon and Lord Goff were left to give the only substantive judgments. Lord Brandon eschewed narrow literal interpretations. He said: 'In my opinion, the provisions contained in s.1(2)(a) of the Act of 1969 must be given a broad and liberal construction which gives full effect to their legislative purpose.'

Lord Brandon confirmed that the expression 'is being' referred to 'a continuing, rather than an instant, situation'. He went on to confirm that the court must consider 'a continuing situation of one or other of the kinds described in s.1(2)(a) exists, . . . at the point of time immediately before the process of protecting the child concerned is first put into motion.' He said further that in considering the question, the Juvenile Court 'must look both at the situation as it is at that point of time and also at the situation as it has been in the past: how far back in the past must depend on the facts of any particular case.'

As for the need to look into the future when considering the 'proper development' ground, Lord Brandon said the court should do this, 'but only in a hypothetical way of looking to see whether the situation which began earlier and was still continuing at the point of time immediately before the process of protecting the child was put into motion would, if that process had not been put into motion, have been likely to continue further.'

Applying these principles to the facts of *Re D*, Lord Brandon concluded that the Juvenile Court 'had ample material' on which to find the condition satisfied in respect of both the child's proper development and his health. 'Each situation', he said, 'could have been avoided if the mother had not persisted in taking excessive narcotic drugs throughout her pregnancy.' He went on to consider immaterial the fact that the cause of the problem and the possibility of avoiding it dated back to the time before birth.

Lord Goff, while agreeing that the Juvenile Court had been entitled to find the case proved, and giving a shorter judgment than Lord Brandon, put greater emphasis on the need for the Juvenile Court to look into the future when considering the proper development condition, and defined the court's obligation rather differently. The magistrates were, he said 'bound to consider whether . . . there is an existing likelihood that the state of affairs revealed by those past events will continue into the future, in order to decide whether the necessary continuum exists at the relevant time.'

Thus Lord Goff did not say, as Lord Brandon said, that the look into the future should be hypothetical, on the basis that proceedings had not commenced. In formulating the requirement to consider the future in relation to the 'proper development' condition as he did, Lord Goff appears to support the duplication of the question which arises in any event for the magistrates in the separate 'care and control' test. Lord Brandon's statement of the correct approach should, therefore, I suggest, be preferred.

To illustrate his view of the Juvenile Court's duty to consider the future in relation to the proper development condition, Lord Goff gave as an example the case of an alcoholic mother who, having damaged her unborn baby through drinking, shortly before the birth becomes a confirmed teetotaller. Following the birth, Lord Goff went on, the local authority could not in that event sustain the proper development condition.

Lord Goff's illustration was hypothetical and not intended, perhaps, to be scrutinised too closely. Even so, the hardened

Juvenile Court practitioner might, faced with such a case in practice, suspect the presence of recklessness in a Juvenile Court's finding that a long-standing alcoholic would be likely to be associated with copper-bottomed abstinence after a matter of a few months. If Lord Goff's illustration were truly apt, the difference between failure to sustain the 'proper development' condition and success, might be, surmise suggests, a single proved or admitted lapse on the parent's part following the birth.

While of great assistance in respect of general principles, the reported cases do not offer help with all situations. One situation which can arguably be the basis for care proceedings on the 'proper development' grounds is that where the child, although not so far showing evidence of damage, has been repeatedly exposed to violence between parents by being present. Such exposure might be regarded as amounting to neglect of 'proper development' or 'health'. Yet more than in some other categories of case, perhaps, emergency removal would not normally be justified prior to proceedings.

Decisions to institute care proceedings are not, of course, just a matter of concluding whether or not a case can be made to fit within statutory boundaries for proceedings. That is a part of the process, but another part must be the relation of the case being considered to professional assumptions as to what are acceptable levels of child care. Thus a loss of temper by a parent coupled with a single act of inappropriate physical assault, for instance, kicking a toddler in the leg or bottom without causing more than a bruise, is unlikely in itself to give rise to care proceedings, although technically 'ill-treatment' has been committed.

Even where standards of care become unacceptable, before care proceedings are considered it may well be that social work intervention and, possibly, voluntary care is offered. Emergency removals under Place of Safety Orders should, likewise, be cautiously considered and should never be employed as a convenient way of commencing the care proceedings process. I have no doubt that proceedings without initial removal are too seldom begun.

Where proceedings are authorised, if the local authority feels the burden of a heavy weight of responsibility when mounting difficult Juvenile Court cases, despite the warm benign wind brought by *M v Westminster City Council* and *Re D*, the reason may sometimes partly lie in the rules of evidence.

Problems of evidence

Evidence is and must be, save where otherwise agreed between the parties, given orally in Juvenile Court care proceedings. The small exceptions to this rule, in particular with regard to descriptive medical evidence and school attendance records, are really drops in the ocean of Juvenile Court evidence. In contested cases most evidence is delivered live from the witness box.

This can make for distortion in those cases where the evidence consists of an accumulation of incidents, none of them major, over a long period of time. A blow by blow assembly of the history from a witness risks overwhelming the Bench, hampered by the lack of written statements, especially if the irrelevant has not been painstakingly weeded out. An attempt to construct the essence of the history through a short impressionistic sketch may leave, on the other hand, little that seems solid and tangible to persuade the court.

Is it right that the Juvenile Court in care cases should not have the advantage High Court judges have of being able to read affidavits and reports filed previously and to refer to them during oral evidence?

A further uncertainty in the Juvenile Court is the extent to which allegations made by children to social workers and other professional witnesses can be repeated in the witness box as admissible 'hearsay' evidence of the truth of allegations. Such allegations may be against a parent who denies their truth. In practice efforts are made to spare children the ordeal of giving evidence. So children do not often give evidence unless they wish to, and courts tend to admit this form of hearsay evidence despite the difficulty of testing it. The present case law suggests that a witness's statement as to what one parent has alleged against another is not admissable.

The problems for local authority cases are magnified when, after a case has resulted in an order, there is a subsequent application on behalf of the child—or under the Children and Young Persons (Amendment) Act 1986, partly in force since 1 August 1988, on behalf of the parent—to discharge the order.

Imagine a possible scenario. A baby is admitted several times to hospital because of illness during her first months of life. The causes of illness are unclear, but a final admission suggests strongly to the hospital paediatrician that the child has suffered brain damage due to violent shaking. This diagnosis, together with other concerns, gives rise to care proceedings. Ultimately the medical and other evidence results in a care order, despite conflicting medical evidence from another paediatrician called in on the parent's behalf after the child's discharge from hospital. After several months the baby is placed with foster parents with a view to adoption. There is then an application to discharge the care order on the parents' behalf.

Here the local authority lawyer must consider very carefully what evidence should be called in opposition to the application to discharge the care order. Should *all* the earlier oral evidence be called, as well as evidence of what has occurred since the care order. Putting the question more simply: should there be a complete re-run of the original care proceedings case with some extra up-dating evidence poured on top?

It may be argued that the later Bench should treat the earlier Bench as having made findings on the earlier evidence. But all the earlier Bench did was make the finding that the 'proper development' condition was made out, and then exercised its discretion to make a care order. The Bench's findings of fact would not have been recorded or disclosed.

Thus, not to call the hospital paediatrician responsible for the original diagnosis may render the local authority's case vulnerable, especially if the parent calls the author of the earlier conflicting medical evidence.

And what to do if the original paediatrician has emigrated or is enjoying a sabbatical year in distant foreign parts? It is understandable, in such cases, that a local authority may, at some stage, choose the safer haven of the High Court, where evidence once filed is filed for all time, and where findings of fact are enshrined within judgments of which transcripts can subsequently be obtained.

The winds of change

The winds of change are certainly blowing around the Juvenile Court care proceedings arena. They have been blowing there for some time. There has been the grant to the court of the power to appoint guardians ad litem to represent children's interests. There has been the extension of legal aid to parents in care proceedings in their own right. Both were long overdue reforms. Now, since 1 August 1988, the Children and Young Persons (Amendment) Act 1986 gives parents other than non-marital fathers full 'party status', and gives grandparents the right to apply to the court to become parties.

Other far-ranging changes will come with the Children Bill. The problems of investigation, assessment and evidence inherent in child abuse proceedings, however, will continue, and while legislative reform will remove some problems, others may be expected to arise from the reforms themselves. It is to be hoped that overall the business of child protection will be buttressed, and that the availability of wardship in the High Court for the most difficult cases will not be curtailed.

References

1. DHSS (1985). Review of Child Care Law, HMSO, London.
2. The Law on Child Care and Family Services (1987).
3. *Re G* [1987] 1 FLR 310.
4. *M v Westminster City Council* [1985] FLR 325.
5. *Re D* [1987] 1 FLR 422 HL
6. *Re G* [1987] 1 WLR 1461.

CHAPTER 10

Child Sexual Abuse

A model for interagency
collaboration in the
diagnosis, investigation
and management, including
an epidemiological review
of child sexual abuse

GRAHAM ANTHONY

Detective sergeant

JANE JENKINS

Child abuse co-ordinator

DR JANE WATKEYS

Consultant community
paediatrician

Introduction

Child Sexual Abuse has been increasingly recognised over the last few years and in 1987 there was much controversy surrounding the diagnosis, investigation and management of this condition. Most cases of child sexual abuse are still diagnosed as a result of specific allegations and few are picked up as a result of changes in the child's behaviour or on routine physical examination. Overall, society has been slow to acknowledge the existence of any form of abuse of children. The existence and acknowledgement of sexual abuse has only occurred recently.

As with other forms of abuse in childhood, it is essential that all agencies involved in child care work together as a team. Close collaboration ensures that the sexually abused child is protected, receives the necessary treatment and support, and that any offender is brought to justice.

This paper outlines the extent of the problem as identified nationally, and locally. It outlines the procedures that have been developed in South Glamorgan in the identification, investigation and support to families where child sexual abuse has occurred.

Definition of child sexual abuse

Varying definitions of child sexual abuse have been formulated. The definitions used by Health and Social Services Departments tend to differ from the strict legal definition. Kempe and Kempe[1] defined sexual abuse in the following way:

> Sexual abuse is defined as the involvement of dependent, developmentally, immature children and adolescents in sexual activities they do not truly comprehend, to which they are unable to give informed consent or that violate the social taboos of family roles.

In South Glamorgan the definition used is as follows:

> Sexual abuse is defined as the involvement of any child under the age of 16 years in sexual activities within the family, or extended family, or with activity which involves a person known to a child.
> It includes:
> (1) children who have experienced attempted or actual intercourse or other inappropriate genital or oral contact, eg with activities such as fondling, mutual masturbation.
> (2) Exposure to illegal or otherwise inappropriate sexual activities such as involvement in pornographic photography, or exposure to sexually explicit material.

Both of these apply whether or not the activity is initiated by the child and whether or not there is any discernible harmful outcome.

The definition would include, rape, buggery, unlawful sexual intercourse, and incest, as defined by the law. Many legal definitions are very narrow, eg incest. Incest applies only to acts of sexual intercourse between a man and a women within certain prohibited relationships; namely a man with a woman who he knows to be his daughter, sister, half-sister, mother or grand-daughter, a woman over the age of 16 years with a man who is her father, brother or half-brother, son or grandfather. Illegitimate children are covered by this law, but not adopted and step children.

Incidence of child sexual abuse

It is impossible to know the true incidence of child sexual abuse, as many cases remain undiagnosed. Many studies have been carried out over the last 30 years, into the incidence and prevalence of child sexual abuse. However, information about the true incidence is difficult to obtain because the definition of child sexual abuse has varied from study to study, the methods of carrying out the studies have varied enormously—some being retrospective studies with groups of students, others have looked at the cases referred for professional help.

Equally, it is difficult to know whether the incidence of child sexual abuse is actually increasing, or whether the apparent increase is due to increasing recognition. International comparisons in the incidence and prevalance of child sexual abuse are equally impossible for the reasons given above. The involvement of children in adult sexuality is nothing new, but it became especially shocking as the ideology of childhood innocence took root in the middle classes in late Victorian times. It is worth remembering that incest is a relatively new criminal offence and was only put on the statute books in 1908 and followed concern because of increased reporting of sexual abuse in childhood in the 1890s.[2] Freud[3] at the end of the 19th century was struck by the frequency of complaints by his female patients of having been sexually assaulted as children usually by their fathers. Tardieu[4] and Bernard[5] in the late 19th century, documented the high incidence of sexual abuse of children revealed by physical examinations.

Evidence from adults of child sexual contacts is far in excess of what was formerly believed. The evidence of this comes from questioning of adults about their childhood recollections.

Weinberg[6] in 1955 estimated that there was one case of incest per million persons per year in English-speaking countries. Ferracuti[7] in 1972 estimated that there were between one and five cases of incest per million persons every year throughout the world. Criminal statistics provide little insight into the incidence of child sexual abuse, and represent perhaps only the more serious end of the spectrum, eg in 1984, 73 persons were tried in the Crown Courts for unlawful sexual intercourse with a girl under 13 years, and 135 for unlawful sexual intercourse with a girl under 16. In the same year 139 persons appeared on the charge of incest. NSPCC statistics[8] using child abuse registers in 11 different areas, found incidence rates per thousand under the age of 17 years of 0.27 in 1985 and 0.57 in 1986. Mrazek et al[9] in 1977–8, on a postal questionnaire to professionals, ie 1599 family doctors, police surgeons, paediatricians and child psychiatrists, found an overall incidence of 3/1000 children recognised as being sexually abused during childhood.

Russell[10] had shown an incidence of sexual abuse of 24% in female college students in the USA, Russell interviewed 4ju wiiiiiin and found an incidence of sexual abuse of 16% within the family and 31% outside the family before the age of 18 years, ie an overall incidence of 24%. However, this study was retrospective and had a 50% refusal rate. Finkelhor[11] found 19% of female college students had been exposed to some form of extra-familial sexual abuse, but only 9% of male students. However, only 1% had experienced genital contact.

Nash and West[12] studied 148 female students and found 25% of respondents reported physical sexual experiences.

In the Mori Survey (Baker and Duncan)[13] of just over 2000 people in 1985, 10% of the subjects interviewed reported being sexually abused before the age of 16 years, ie 12% of females and 8% of males. However, as with Finkelhor's study a similar number had experienced genital contact and in the Mori Poll 1 in 370 had experienced intercourse.

In studies of incidence there is a very definite pattern that girls appear more frequently abused than boys in the order of 3 : 1. However, within family settings boys and girls appear to be equally involved. Some authors believe that boys overall may be sexually abused as commonly as girls, and this may be particularly true in the pre-school years. This concept is based on the following (a) 85% of child molesters were abused as children and (b) most confirmed paedophiles who abuse many children outside the family prefer young males. It is generally accepted that most abusers are males (95%).

In incest, father–daughter incest is certainly the best documented form of incest; Finkelhor[11] thought 60% of incestuous relationships involved a father and/or stepfather, while Roberge concluded 78% of reported incest involves fathers and daughters.

South Glamorgan has a child population under the age of 14 years of approximately 77 000. There are approximately 5800 live births each year.

The number of reported cases of child sexual abuse has increased over the last few years, whereas the incidence of other forms of abuse has changed very little over the last 4–5 years. These cases of child sexual abuse refer to cases referred via the child abuse procedure and refer to children abused within the family.

The incidence of child sexual abuse in South Glamorgan is much greater if children abused outside the family are included. In 1987 114 children were examined by the author where child sexual abuse was suspected. There will also be children who would have been examined by police surgeons and other paediatricians, but this would be a small number (Table 1).

**Table 1. *Area Child Protection Committee*
Referrals via the child abuse procedure
January 1987–December 1987**

Category of Referral	Physical: non-accidental injury	Neglect/failure to thrive	Emotional abuse	Sexual abuse	Potential abuse	Not substantiated following investigation	Total
Jan	7	1	—	7	3	6	24
Feb	3	—	1	7	4	6	21
Mar	5	—	—	8	5	20	38
Apr	4	—	2	2	5	7	20
May	8	—	—	3	7	13	31
Jun	10	1	—	5	8	23	47
Jul	12	—	—	4	3	16	35
Aug	3	1	—	2	5	6	17
Sep	4	2	—	1	3	11	21
Oct	3	—	—	4	6	8	21
Nov	1	2	—	5	11	16	35
Dec	3	1	—	5	3	11	23
Tot	63	8	3	53	63	143	333
%	19	2	1	16	19	43	100

In 1987 there appeared to be an overall reported incidence of child sexual abuse before the age of 14 years of 1.5/1000 of child population.

This shows an apparent increase from 1986, with an incidence then of 0.5/1000 of child population. This incidence is the same as that reported by the NSPCC in 1986.

Medical findings in child sexual abuse
presenting features

The medical examination has an important part to play in the diagnosis of child sexual abuse. Nevertheless it is only one part of the investigation into child sexual abuse and often the least helpful.

There has been much controversy surrounding who should carry out the medical examination and the experience necessary to do this.[14,15] Another area of controversy is the meaning of different findings on physical examination, eg the anal dilatation test, and the significance of a medical examination that reveals no abnormal findings.

It is first necessary to be clear as to the purpose of the medical examination. A medical examination is carried out for the following reasons:

(a) To collect evidence to substantiate the information given by the child. Linked with this would be the necessity in certain circumstances to take samples for forensic and bacteriological investigation.
(b) To detect and treat any sequelae in the victim.
(c) To assess the health, growth and development of the child.
(d) To reassure and allay anxiety in the child about what may or may not have happened to him/her.

This indicates that any medical examination should be more than a look at the genitalia. The assessment must include a history of physical health, as well as development and behaviour, measurement of height and weight and full physical examination. Usually forensic specimens are taken if and when appropriate. However, White et al[16] and Goodwin et al[17] describe a systematic approach to the medical examination, which should always include routine testing for syphilis, gonorrhoea and trichomonas.

Enos et al[18] found positive findings in only 40% of cases. Hobbs and Wynne[19] state that 40-50% of boys and girls examined have anal abnormalities, and Wynne has stated that 50-60% of sexually abused children will have signs if the examination is done carefully. However, the absence of positive findings does not exclude a diagnosis of sexual abuse, because many children have been subjected to acts of fondling, mutual masturbation and other forms of indecent assault, which leave no clinical signs.

Fifty per cent of all sodomy cases manifest a normal appearing anus because the anus is capable of accommodating large hard stools the size of which could equal the average diameter of that of an adult erect penis which would be 3.5 cm.

Other indications that child sexual abuse may have occurred include changes in behaviour either at home or in a school setting as well as the development of non-specific symptoms such as enuresis (bed wetting), abdominal pain and encopresis (soiling).

Frequently there is an impression that the child is more sexually aware than would be expected, and occasionally the child may make sexual advances to the examining doctor.

Frequently medical examinations are not carried out because of adult anxiety, ie adults see the medical examination as another assault. To alleviate this anxiety it is essential that the medical examination should be carried out sensitively, should never be forced on a child and the child should be constantly reassured. Children should always be medically examined as the examination remains an important part of the investigation into child sexual abuse, despite its limitations

Table 2

	Boys	Girls	Total
1986	3	31	34
1987	29	85	114
1988 (first quarter)	13	17	30
	45 (26%)	133 (74%)	178

Table 3. Presence and/or absence of physical changes of the genitalia

1986	Girls 31	vaginal changes	14 (45%)
		anal changes	0
		behaviour changes	0
	Boys 3	anal changes	1 (33%)
		behaviour changes	1
	Total number with no change		19
1987	Girls 85	vaginal changes	41 (48%)
		anal changes	7
		other physical findings	2
	Boys 29	anal changes	6 (20%)
		behaviour changes	2
	Total number with no change		64
1988	Girls 17	vaginal changes	8 (47%)
		anal changes	3
		behaviour changes	0
	Boys 13	anal changes	4 (30%)
		behaviour changes	1
	Total number with no change		18

Equally, if one child in a family has been abused, other children in that household should be examined. A study in South Glamorgan indicated that 60% of siblings had also been abused.

In South Glamorgan, the author has examined a total of 178 children between 1986 and the first quarter of 1988 (see Table 2). The results of these examinations are shown in Table 3.

These figures show an overall change in genitalia—vaginal in girls in 47% cases, and anal changes in girls in 7.5% of cases. In boys, anal changes were noted in 24%. Anal changes were noted overall in 11% of cases. Goodwin has reported that other medical conditions will be found in 20% of cases. In 6 cases there were other changes noted, but in no child was either spermatozoa or evidence of sexually transmitted disease detected. In no case was there forensic corroboration. The only positive finding was the isolation of thread worms in one case.

Twenty-two cases were unsubstantiated, and of the remainder 58% were within the family. As one would expect, the younger the children, the less likely sexual intercourse had taken place apart from anal intercourse in young boys. This is in keeping with the types of abuse that occur at each developmental stage.

Age distribution

The NSPCC had reported that during the years 1985/86 the mean age of sexually abused children was 10 years 2 months, and that 18% of sexually abused children registered in 1986 were less than 5 years.[8]

Wynne[19] found that half the children studied were under 5 years old. In South Glamorgan, of the 178 children examined the youngest child involved was less than 2 years and the oldest 17 years (she was mentally handicapped). The mean age of children examined was 11 years—21% of girls and 33% of boys were abused before the age of 5 years.

This agrees with previous studies that indicate that boys tend to be abused at a younger age (Table 4)

Table 4. Age distribution of child sexual abuse

Age	Boys	Girls
<5 years	15 (33%)	29 (21%)
6–10 years	18 (40%)	66 (49%)
11 years +	12 (27%)	38 (28%)
Total	45	133

Presentation

The majority of cases presented as a complaint made either by the child, or member of family, school or neighbour (Table 5). Very few were detected because of changes in behaviour. In an even smaller number, ie 2, was the sexual abuse detected on routine examination. This is a very different pattern from that reported from other parts of the country, eg Leeds, where it is reported that only 20% of children are seen following a clear disclosure. In South Glamorgan 66% of children were examined following a definite complaint of sexual abuse.

The report by Baker and Duncan[13] confirmed that sexual abuse of children is not confined to a small peripheral section of the community, but that it is proportionally evident across all socioeconomic classes and area of residence. However, some studies

Table 5. Presentation in child sexual abuse

Complaint made by child/family/school	118 (66%)
Behaviour changes in child noted by school/parents	36 (20%)
Changes found on medical examination	2 (1%)
Children examined as siblings of abused child and children of offender	22 (13%)
Total	178

have shown that child sexual abuse tends to occur in the poorest and most overcrowded of city districts, or in the sparsely populated rural areas, where families have restricted access to a wider social network. There is increasing evidence to suggest child sexual abuse occurs in all strata of society but the frequency is not equal in all social classes as measured by father's occupation, family income and parents' educational attainments.

There is equally conflicting evidence as to whether child sexual abuse occurs more frequently in certain ethnic groups. However, Bentovim et al[20] found that referrals for treatment showed a predominance of lower social class groups among the parents.

In South Glamorgan, although cases have been found in all strata of society, there is a definite predominence of cases in the lower social classes, and cases appear to be found in greater numbers in certain areas of the City, ie in the poorer more deprived areas of the City of Cardiff and Vale of Glamorgan (Figure 1). However, like Bentovim's data, this is based on reported cases and not on a general survey.

Offenders

139 children of the 178 children medically examined were definitely found to have been abused. Of these 57% had been associated with family members (Table 6).

The study of the offenders shows a very similar pattern to that reported by Russell.[10] She indicated that 40% of incestuous child abuse occurred within the nuclear family, and this is shown clearly here. The data from South Glamorgan does indicate that uncle and brother incestuous relationships are common.

From the extrafamilial abuse here only 12% was perpetrated by strangers, a figure very similar to that reported by Russell, ie 15%.

Russell looked at the different offenders, combining extra- and intrafamilial child sexual abuse and reported that 11% was with

Figure 1. Incidence of child abuse and distribution throughout South Glamorgan (City of Cardiff health facilities)

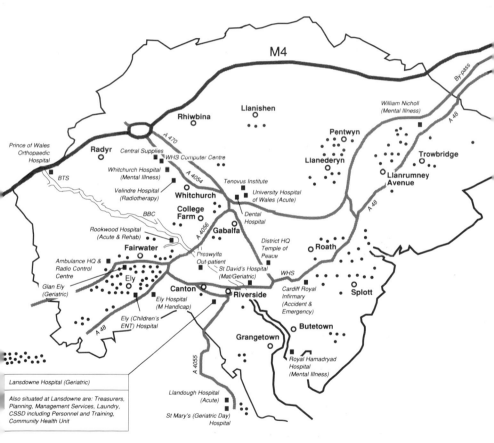

• Represents one incident of Child Abuse

Table 6. Offenders

Family Members		
Stepfather/father/cohabitee	49	
Uncle	8	
Grandfather	4	
Cousins	3	73
Brothers	8	
Other family members		
Mother	1	
Outside Family		
Neighbours	28 + 12 involving sex rings	
Foster home	1	
Others—Stranger Abuse	7	66
Boys in school	10	
Offender—no definite conclusive evidence	8	

total strangers, 29% with relatives and 60% with persons known but unrelated to the victims. In this small study in South Glamorgan, 49% of offenders were well known but unrelated to victims, whereas 5% were total strangers. The different patterns may reflect that the study in South Glamorgan is based on referrals following in the majority of cases complaints of abuse.

Interestingly only one mother appears to have been involved in sexual abuse and this involved mother/stepson. Groth has argued that the number of female perpetrators is grossly underestimated and that 5% of female children and 20% of male children who are abused are abused by a woman.

Finkelhor[11] has estimated that boys are more likely to be victimised extrafamilialy and this is seen in this case. Eleven of the 12 children involved with the 'sex ring' were boys, thus supporting the author's findings.

Police investigated 113 cases, which resulted in 64 cases being prosecuted (56%). This does not include cautions. Twelve cases are still under investigation and in 8 cases no prosecution followed because the Crown Prosecution Service decided there was insufficient corroborative evidence, linked to the age of the child victim, and ability to give unsworn evidence, or because the offender was mentally handicapped.

Of the 64 cases where prosecution took place, in 42 cases a custodial sentence was passed. Only 2 alleged offenders have been acquitted. Eight others are still awaiting trial. The majority of offenders had abused 1 child, but 2 had abused more than 5 children.

Table 7. Analysis of offenders—68

No. abusing 1 child	48
No. abusing 2 children	14
No. abusing 3 children	2
No. abusing 4 children	2
No. abusing 5+children	2

Two of the offenders were involved with 'sex rings' and had been involved with 6–8 children.

Of the grandfathers involved in abuse, there was evidence in 3 of the 4 cases that the grandfathers had also been involved with abusing their own children, ie mothers of the presently abused children.

In the families where intrafamilial abuse had occurred 13 mothers had admitted to being sexually abused by their own fathers/or other close family members, ie 10% of mothers admitted to some form of abuse in their childhood.

Information concerning offenders and abuse is not completely available—though 1 offender came from a family in which incest had involved the last 3 generations.

Therefore in summary, the findings in South Glamorgan in incidence show that the age of children tends to follow patterns reported both nationally and in the United States. However, there is little evidence of anal abuse, particularly in young girls, and most of the positive anal findings in young children are found in extra-familial cases. Venereal disease has not been detected and in no case has there been clear forensic evidence, indicating the chronic nature of the condition in the majority of cases, and the frequent delay in presentation.

Sexual abuse usually presents following a complaint from a victim or a member of the family, and it is rare for evidence of abuse to be picked up on routine medical examination.

The Police are informed of all cases, and the prosecution rate is high. Conviction rates are also high with only 2 alleged offenders being found not guilty.

Abnormal physical findings involving the genitalia are found in less than 50% of cases.

Procedures to be followed when a case of child sexual abuse is suspected, either following complaint or following routine medical examination

In 1974 the DHSS[21] recommended that Area Review Committees should be set up. Since then there has been a flow of advice from central and local government concentrating on multidisciplinary co-ordination at the referral, diagnosis and early intervention stage in child abuse. The DHSS Study of Inquiry Reports[22] suggests that the duties of various disciplines involved, ie medicine, education, police, social services, have not been given sufficient attention.

The most recent guidelines from the DHSS[23] concentrate once again on interagency collaboration and defining areas of responsibility. The document also considered the way in which child sexual abuse should be managed. In addition a Home Office circular in 1988, clearly embraces the concept of a police/social work joint investigation.

A variety of different models for investigating child sexual abuse, has been developed in this country and abroad. Examples of these include the specialist child psychiatry team at Great Ormond Street Hospital, the scheme jointly run by Bexley Social Services and the Metropolitan Police[24] in Sidcup, the NSPCC unit at Rochdale, and the multidisciplinary team in Tower Hamlets.[25] Many of these models have been successful but in all of them problems have arisen during the identification of roles for individual professional groups as to who has the key role in investigation and management of cases.[26]

South Glamorgan produced its first procedure for the management of child abuse in 1975—and a procedure for the management of child sexual abuse was introduced in the 1984 Child Abuse booklet. However, practice has moved so fast that the 1984 procedure has rapidly become out of date. This is exciting and encouraging as it implies agencies are having to work differently in cases of sexual abuse in response to an awareness of current research and increased sensitivity to the subject. The procedure model to be introduced in the revised child abuse procedure is illustrated in diagrammatic form (Figure 2). There are two essential elements which characterise this process and make it different from previous procedures. The *first* is the concept of pausing and planning. Workers have become more and more aware that if one is able to plan the intervention, then the trauma experienced by the child is reduced. There may be only one opportunity to help the child; the abused child may retract the allegation if he/she feels threatened or scared. This planned intervention involves close co-operation with workers from other agencies—in particular the police and medical services.

The second important concept is that of joint investigation of a case by the police and social workers.

Figure 2. Child sexual abuse—the investigatory process

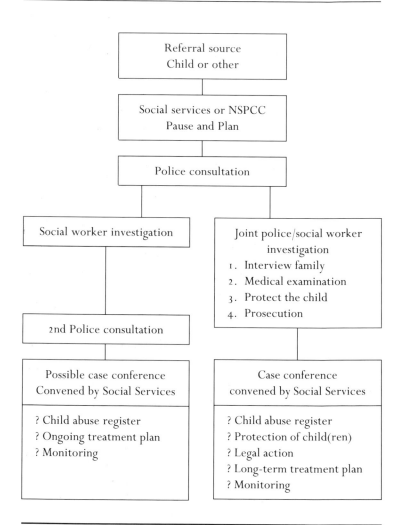

Police role in joint investigation

Cases involving the sexual abuse of children in domestic situations which occur within the South Wales Constabulary area are dealt with in accordance with the agreed procedures which encompass all forms of child abuse.

Whilst the force has a policy of maintaining close liaison with the other agencies who may be involved, it is recognised that the prime responsibility for investigating criminal offences of sexual abuse against children rests firmly with the police. There is, however, a commitment to pre-intervention planning or strategy discussion prior to the start of the investigation, and to both parties, social services and police, being involved at all stages of the investigation.

The procedures require that all allegations are reported to the relevant detective chief inspector who is then responsible for allocating the investigation to a suitably experienced detective officer of normally, not less than the rank of sergeant. He in turn is responsible for liaising with the nominated social worker. The investigating officer and the nominated social worker will form part of an investigating team. Both will be responsible for planning the investigation, updating both services and gaining access to all other relevant information.

Notwithstanding the statutory duty placed upon the police to investigate possible breaches of the criminal law, the investigating officer will at all times be conscious of the welfare of the child.

The first consideration of the investigating officer will be to assess the validity of the complaint, ie to establish whether the complaint has arisen from a disclosure made by the victim or from a third party who suspects that a child has been or is being abused. These sets of circumstances each require quite separate actions and considerations. Evidence from Great Ormond Street[27] would suggest that the complaint is more likely to be true if it originates from the victim rather than from other family members, and this is borne out by the cases investigated within South Glamorgan.

Where a disclosure has been made, it is essential that the offenders are not made aware that a complaint is being investigated by any intervention agency. Consideration must also be given to arresting the abusers in isolation from their family. This ensures that the abusers (a) are unable to cause harm to themselves or others, because if they are forewarned that they are to be arrested for such a socially unacceptable crime, their reaction is unpredictable, and (b) do not see their families' reaction thus placing them in an entrenched position when it comes to interview; and (c) that the families do not witness the arrest because their co-operation with the investigation will be required, ie the medical examination of the siblings and the interview of the spouse.

The intervention team must also consider where and when the children of the family are to be interviewed and examined, and what evidence for care proceedings is already available.

The above considerations apply to both types of referral: (1) those that have arisen from a direct disclosure or (2) those arising indirectly from concerned parties, ie family members, teachers, doctors.

It is important that experienced police personnel should be used to interview the victim, in order to (1) avoid the use of leading questions and (2) ensure that there is no adverse reaction to the victim's story which may destroy any rapport between victim and interviewer, through embarrassment, disbelief or mistrust. It must also be borne in mind that the initial complaint may not be a complete account of the abuse the victim has suffered and may only refer initially to minor sexual acts although far more serious offences may have been committed.

All interviews of juveniles by police officers take place in the presence of an appropriate adult who may be a relative, social worker or teacher. In the case of a relative, the likelihood of him or her becoming emotional or disruptive during the interview must be considered.

In a non-specific referral more time can be taken to plan the intervention. Premature intervention can cause as much stress for the victim of suspected abuse as the abuse itself. Good planning and interagency collaboration can only lead to a more professional therapeutic approach to family intervention, and avoid possible retraction of the complaint.

If the victim is either too young or suffering from a mental or physical defect, and is not capable of making a complaint, the reasons for suspicion must be thoroughly investigated and consideration given to medically examining the child to ascertain whether the suspicion can be substantiated.

Throughout the investigation the officer will continue in his quest for corroboration of the complaints and reliable evidence. Corroboration in most sexual offences is not demanded by law, but is required as a matter of good practice. Part of the corroboration sought will be medical opinion and forensic findings. It must be remembered that medical opinion may support the victim's story, but will not necessarily identify the suspect as being the person responsible. In cases of child sexual abuse within the family, the complaint is often made some time after the last sexual act and forensic corroboration is unusual. However, the possibility of recovering excellent corroborative evidence cannot be discounted, indeed the development of DNA fingerprinting considerably enhances the likelihood of positively identifying the offender.

Although the welfare of children who are the subject of a sexual abuse enquiry will always be uppermost, the issues are not always clearcut and due regard has to be given to the rights of parents or other parties involved.

The social work role in joint investigation

It is important to note that the Social Services Department or the NSPCC have a legal duty to investigate any referral of child abuse as well as the police. It is clear that the main focus of the police role is to collect the evidence which may eventually lead to prosecution of the alleged abuser. The social worker intervention will aim to focus on the therapeutic needs of the victim. If it is accepted that therapy can begin from the point of disclosure then the social worker's presence is essential throughout the investigating process. In the past the process of collecting evidence and the need to initiate therapy have been seen as essentially in conflict.

The joint police/social work investigation model aims to eradicate any conflict by early planning which will lead to a clear definition of roles and an understanding of the various tasks which need to be achieved if the healing process is to begin and the abuser is to be brought to justice.

The primary social work role is the duty to protect the child and any siblings. This will involve assessing family members' ability to care and protect the child from further abuse. To protect the child victim by means of a Place of Safety Order has to be given serious consideration and experience has shown that it only needs to be used where the child appears unprotected in the family home. In South Glamorgan, it has only been necessary to take Place of Safety Orders in 15% of cases already described.

In supporting the child and family members the social worker will seek to validate the child's position and aim to give back to the child some control over events. As has already been stated, there is evidence to suggest that early planning and close working together by the two main agencies involved in the investigation reduces the trauma for the child and the long-term effects. This process, however, which should be initiated during the investigation, may take months or years to complete. Long-term treatment of the child, siblings and other family members will clearly need to continue long after the police involvement is terminated. The point of early planning and collaboration is that it should enhance the process which will enable the victim to become a survivor.

Conclusion

This chapter outlines the method by which child sexual abuse is dealt with in an area of South Wales. It highlights the importance of interagency collaboration at every stage in diagnosis, investigation and management of child sexual abuse cases. For this to be successful there must be trust and respect between the different agencies, and this is being enhanced by the setting up of joint training programmes for police and social services. There must be co-operation and collaboration from the point of referral, or suspicion of sexual abuse, and working together must continue throughout the whole investigation process.

References

1. Kempe, R S, and Kempe, C H (1978) *Child Abuse*. Fontana/ Open Books.
2. Johnson, A (1886) *Lectures on the Surgery of Childhood*. London.
3. Masson, J M (1984) *Freud. The Assault on Truth. Freud's suppression of the seduction theory*. Faber, London.
4. Tardieu, A (1878) *Attentats aux moeurs*. Ballière et fils, Paris.
5. Bernard, P (1886) *Des Attentats à la pudeur sur les petites filles*. Octave Doris, Paris.
6. Weinberg, S G (1955) revised 1976. *Incest Behaviour*. Citadel Press, Secaucus, New Jersey.
7. Ferracuti, F (1972) Incest between father and daughter in Resnick, H L and Wolfgang, M E (eds.) *Sexual Behaviours*, pp 169–83.
8. Creighton, S J (1987) Child abuse in 1986 initial findings from the NSPCC Register Research, NSPCC, London, (Research Briefing No. 8).
9. Mrazek, P J, Lynch, M and Bentovim, A (1983) Sexual abuse of children in the United Kingdom. *Child Abuse and Neglect*, pp 147–53.

10. Russell, D E H (1983) The incidence and prevalence of intrafamilial and extrafamilial sexual abuse of female children. *Child Abuse and Neglect*, 7. pp. 133–146.

11. Finkelhor, D (1979) *Sexually Victimized Children*. The Free Press, New York.

12. Nash, C L and West, D J (1988) Sexual molestation of young girls in West, D J (ed.) *Sexual Victimisation*. Gower, Aldershot, 1–92.

13. Baker, A and Duncan, S (1985) Child sexual abuse, a study of prevalence in Great Britain, *Child Abuse and Neglect*, 9, 4.

14. Hobbs, C J and Wynne, J (1986) Buggery in childhood—a common syndrome of child abuse. *Lancet*, ii, 92–6.

15. Hobbs, C J and Wynne, J (1987) Management of sexual abuse. *Archives of Diseases of Childhood*, 62 (11), 1182–8.
    Roberts, R (1987) Commentary. *Archives of Diseases of Childhood*, 62 (11), 1193–5.

16. White *et al* (1983) Sexually transmitted diseases in sexually abused children. *Paediatrics*, 72, 16–20.

17. Goodwin, J, Willett, A and Jackson, R (1982) Medical care of male and female incest victims and their parents. Incest victims and their families. Goodwin J (ed) pp 35–9. J Wright, Boston (1982).

18. Enos, W F, Conrath, T B and Byer, J C (1986) Forensic evaluation of the sexually abused child. *Paediatrics*, 78, 385–98.

19. Hobbs, C J and Wynne, J (1987) Child sexual abuse—an increasing rate of diagnosis. *Lancet*, 837–840.

20. Bentovim, A, Boston, P and van Elburg, A (1989) Child sexual abuse—children and families referred to a treatment project and the effects of intervention. *British Medical Journal*, 295, 1453–7.

21. DHSS Memorandum of Guidance (1974) LASSL 9740 13/CMO 97408.

22. DHSS (1982) A Study of Inquiry Reports 1973–1981.

23. DHSS (1988) Child Abuse—Working Together. DHSS Guidance issued under cover of HC (88) 38/LAC (88) 10.

24. Bexley Social Services/Metropolitan Police (1987) Joint Investigation.

25. Hall, A and Harries, R J (1985) The development of a multidisciplinary approach to the assessment and management of child sexual abuse in an inner city Health District. *Health Trends*, 20 (2), 39–43.

26. Furniss, T (1988) *Surveying Child Sexual Abuse — Principal Ways and Practical Problems in a Multiprofessional Approach.* Routledge and Kegan Paul, London.

27. Bentovim, A, Teron A *et al* (1988) *Child Sexual Abuse within the Family. Assessment and Treatment.* Bristol, Wright.

The Metropolitan Police Force Response to Child Abuse within the Family: Principles and Code of Practice

Reproduced with the permission of the Metropolitan Police

Prepared by the Metropolitan Police Working Party
on Child Abuse (1987) under the chairmanship of
Detective Chief Superintendent A Kilkerr.

The Code of Practice
is founded on the following principles

1. To pursue a policy reflecting an intention to protect and care for the victim, rehabilitate the family and deal with the offender.

2. To maintain the impetus of the multi-agency approach as laid down in the Force Strategy.

3. To provide a Force response to child abuse which ensures the most effective use of resources in conjunction with local authority social services departments.

4. Continuously to develop investigative techniques to deal with offenders and to enable officers to overcome perceived or real constraints upon investigation and prosecution.

Index to Code of Practice

Code of Practice

1. GENERAL

1.1
Resources

Enhanced support, care and concern for victims of crime is one of the Force goals. It is within this context that the issue of child abuse has to be recognised with resources being made available to combat and prevent harm to this vulnerable section of the community.

1.2
Definition

Child abuse needs to be understood in all its guises, it includes neglect and emotional abuse as well as physical and sexual abuse. Police must be sensitive to the nature of child abuse across the class spectrum whilst being aware of national, cultural and ethnic differences in families.

1.3
Multi-Agency approach

The Metropolitan Police is pledged to support multi-agency co-operation, which is the cornerstone in the prevention and treatment of child abuse.

1.4
Emergency Powers

Police emergency powers to remove a child to a place of safety should only be invoked where there is an immediate risk to the health and safety of the child. In all other circumstances removal of a child should take place only after consultation with the social services department.

1.5
Prosecution of Offenders

The decision to institute criminal proceedings against offenders remains with the police. However, consideration should be given to the views of those participating at case conferences (see Home Office Circular 179/76, paragraphs

16–18 at Appendix A). Where a conference recommends prosecution and there is sufficient evidence to justify this, police should prefer charges accordingly. Where however there is doubt as to the sufficiency of the evidence available, the conference should be informed that the matter will be referred to the Crown Prosecution Service. (See paragraph 8.5 regarding decisions of case conferences.)

1.6
Monitoring

Procedures will be monitored so that best practice will be maintained. Such monitoring should be undertaken locally by a multi-agency sub-committee, with police representation, held under the auspices of the Area Review Committee and supplemented by a central policy reference point in the Community Involvement Policy Unit (TO30) of New Scotland Yard.

1.7
Policy
Decisions

Cases where a policy decision is required should be referred to the Area Detective Chief Superintendent, who may seek advice from TO30 Policy Unit where necessary.

1.8
Criteria
for decision

The protection of the child is the paramount consideration, therefore all the options of response should be considered before deciding on a specific course of action.

Attention must be given to obtaining information regarding previous and potential risk to the child, in addition to gathering evidence for care and/or criminal proceedings. In deciding a course of action consideration will be given to those criteria which best facilitate the treatment options for the victim, family and offender.

1.9
Location of
investigation

It is Force policy that whenever possible there must be an essential shift of responsibility for investigating allegations of child abuse from where the offences took place to the Local Authority Area where the child resides. In such cases this will ensure that the therapeutic needs of the child and the family are addressed in close liaison with the social workers who are responsible for the welfare of the victim. In those cases where investigations on other Divisions or the Force Areas are required, police and social services at the location of the allegation will discuss the circumstances and formally hand over to the victim's local police and social services' managers, who will decide how the incident is to be investigated. This fundamental change from basing the investigation where the offence occurs, to where the child resides, is made in the best interests of the child.

2. INVESTIGATION

2.1
Child Abuse Teams

The Metropolitan Police recognises the need for a core investigative procedure, based on a joint-agency approach, bringing together police officers and social workers into a single investigative team responsible for dealing with all aspects of the investigation, including those traditionally dealt with separately. It is therefore recommended that child abuse teams comprising police and social services should be established across the Metropolitan Police District to investigate all cases of child abuse, and to deal with care and protection of children at risk.

2.2

Area Deputy Assistant Commissioners will ensure that consultation takes place at Area Review Committee level with Directors of Social Services and other agency managers, to mutually agree the channels through which allegations can be processed and joint investigations activated when necessary. This will ensure that police response to child abuse corresponds with both borough requirements and Force policy.

2.3
Specialist Officers

Joint investigations of child abuse cases will only be conducted by those trained and who have been selected for the task. Subject to continued suitability, selected officers should expect to undertake these duties for a period not less than two years, with the express intention of fostering trusting relationships between police, social services and other agencies.

2.4
Selection of team

Investigators must be identified on the basis of their investigative skills, sensitivity and awareness of the victims and their families' needs. Officers should have the ability to work in inter-agency teams, undertaking tasks on a role rather than rank related basis and need not necessarily be selected exclusively from Youth and Community Section and Detective Officers. The compilation of such teams should, whenever possible and practicable, be established on pre-arranged male and female ratios in liaison with the local authority social services departments and, where appropriate, the National Society for the Prevention of Cruelty to Children. These teams will address child abuse and will work together, under the supervision of the Detective Inspector, with their social services counterparts.

2.5
Welfare of
individuals

In view of the stressful nature of this type of work, supervisors must closely monitor the effects on individual officers, provide necessary support and guidance, and ensure that additional staff are prepared through training to supplement the team if the need arises.

2.6

Where there is a low incidence of reported child abuse, consideration should be given to nominating specific individuals for training to undertake the police response from within existing divisional resources, supervised by the divisional Detective Inspector. This should only be done in consultation with the local social services department. Such policy decisions must be recorded, agreed and reviewed annually at Area Headquarters level.

2.7
Police
Co-ordinator

A police child abuse co-ordinator, generally at Detective Chief Inspector rank, will be appointed to liaise with the social services and other agencies on an individual case basis and must be involved in the decisions as to future courses of action during investigations. The police co-ordinator's responsibility will encompass the shared decision making process as to whether investigations will be conducted by police, social services, or jointly. There will be selectivity in the need for joint investigation with social workers, as many cases may be better resolved purely by social work intervention. (See para 1.8 — criteria for decision) The decision must be fully explained and recorded in the crime book and on the case papers. The supervision and co-ordination of investigations will therefore be more direct.

3. TRAINING
3.1

Area Commander (Support) will be responsible for initiating and arranging local training requirements in conjuction with senior officials of their social services departments, and other agencies concerned.

3.2

This must be a joint venture of the police and social services including other agency workers where necessary. Ideally, there should be a balance between police and social workers with an equal number of male and female students not exceeding twelve per course.

3.3

Trainers should be identified from within existing police and social services resources using personnel who have already gained experience in this field and who show an ability to share information and motivate students. Developmental instruction should be given according to individual needs in order to maintain an acceptable Force standard. Training should follow the same core course, syllabus and common working practices conforming to Force Policy, the main principles and this Code of Practice.

3.4

All operational officers from Constable to Inspector rank will receive a general training to make them fully conversant with the police procedures in response to child abuse and the issues involved in dealing with allegations, in line with the responsibilities of their rank.

3.5
Self awareness

One of the most important areas that joint investigative training needs to address is that of *self awareness*. Unless the students are encouraged to understand fully their own feelings and behaviour, it will be difficult for them to have a clear appreciation of the dilemmas facing the child. The rapport between child and investigators is vital in both investigation and possible later therapy, demanding a trust which has to be maintained with a degree of sensitivity acceptable to all.

3.6
Interviewing techniques

Special attention should be given to improving interviewing skills both with children and their families, as well as the general approaches to evidence collecting.

3.7

Training courses for investigators should also address the issues of child care law as well as current information on child care and abuse. The roles of other agencies and Area Review Committees should also be covered. Experience has shown that the relevant information can be imparted during a seven day course, which should be held on mutually acceptable premises.

4. POLICE ACTION

4.1
Action on receipt of allegation

Whenever child abuse is disclosed to police, with the sole exception of emergency action to safe life and limb, the appropriate police child abuse co-ordinator must be informed as soon as practicable. The co-ordinator will then consult with the social services department through their designated person(s) (and any other agencies directly involved), and where necessary investigators from the appropriate specially trained team will be appointed. Area Detective Chief Superintendents will be responsible for ensuring that arrangements are made and instructions issued, covering procedures to deal with referrals that are received outside the normal working hours of co-ordinators and child abuse teams.

4.2
Emergency Powers

In emergency situations where immediate action is necessary to prevent serious injury to the child, police have power of entry under section 17(1)(e) Police and Criminal Evidence Act 1984, ie to save life or limb, and may remove the child to a place of safety under sections 28(2) and (4) Children and Young Persons Act 1969. When it is necessary to apply for a search warrant under section 40 CYPA 1933 in respect of a named child, consideration must be given to the possibility of other children in the same household being at risk. If such a situation is anticipated applications for warrants should include the phrase 'and any other child or children in the same household'.

4.3

In all cases where child abuse is disclosed, including cases where urgent action has been taken, local and central records must be checked and information obtained passed to the police child abuse co-ordinator. When an officer receives information concerning a child or young person, that officer must complete Form 78 as far as possible and submit it through the appropriate Relief/Detective Inspector to the officer in charge of the local child abuse team, who will be responsible for ensuring that action is taken.

4.4
Interviews

Interviews with and medical examinations of child victims should take place at premises other than a police station. Arrangements with hospitals which make special provision for children may be made and ratified by the Area Detective Chief Superintendents. Ideally some purpose built or adapted accommodation, into which medical examination and video recordings could be incorporated, should be sought.

4.5 Medical Examination

The primary object of the medical examination is to diagnose the patient's physical and mental condition and assess the therapeutic requirements for the future of the child. The obtaining of evidence for proceedings will occur at the same time but must remain as a secondary factor during the examination. There are advantages in joint examination being carried out between a paediatrician and an experienced police surgeon, who as a General Practitioner has considerable experience in dealing with children who have not been abused. That doctor will therefore have a broad knowledge base against which to assist the diagnosis of the abused child. Paediatricians, during the normal course of examination, may wish to call upon the services of a police surgeon to assist them in their diagnosis of suspected child abuse. The police surgeon will then be entitled to a consultancy fee, which is to be claimed in Book 83 omitting the name of the child unless abuse is confirmed when reference must be made to the appropriate Crime Book entry.

4.6 Wards of Court

Whilst the emphasis is on welfare of the child, there will be occasions when this has to be weighed against public interest to protect society, including other children, from the perpetration of crime. An example of how the court balances the child's needs against those of society was given recently in the case of *Re S (Minors)* (Wardship: Police Investigation) [1987] 3 WLR 847 when Booth J said at p 851 F–G:

> The court must take into consideration as a matter of public policy, the need to safeguard not only its wards but other children against the harm they may suffer as a result of recurring crimes by undetected criminals . . . (W)hen balanced against the competing public interest which requires the court to protect society from the perpetration of crime *it could only be in exceptional circumstances that the interest of the individual ward should prevail,*

When the child is made a ward of court then no medical examination or interview can take place without leave of the Family Division of the High Court. Applications to the High Court should be made on behalf of police by lawyers of the Crown Prosecution Service or Solicitors Department. In cases of extreme urgency, for example to secure particulars of an assailant which would assist in his immediate apprehension, necessary leave could be obtained by an officer telephoning directly to the Duty Judge of the High Court via 01-936 6000.

5. VIDEO INTERVIEWING
5.1

The use of video interviewing techniques is vital in reducing the trauma of victims having to repeat their story, although at this time it will not replace written statements for evidential purposes in criminal proceedings. It is essential that the agreement of parents or legal guardians is obtained and that they understand the reasons for and consent to the interview being recorded on video and in writing. As the therapeutic needs of the child take precedence over evidential requirements, the value to the medical and welfare professional of the video interview as an aid to their treatment must be considered. When the video recording is required by police for evidential purposes, the social services department should be made aware of this intention. The video should then be treated as an exhibit and a written summary of its content provided for any future presentation by the Crown Prosecution Service.

5.2
Security of Tapes

All video tapes used in these investigations must be securely stored. Access to them must be restricted and the decision whether or not to allow viewing will depend upon the therapeutic or investigative role of the viewer. Local arrangements may mean that the cassette will be considered the property of police, social services or other agency, and therefore it would be retained and exhibited for court proceedings by an officer from that agency.

6. CHILD AS A WITNESS
6.1
Depositions

In order to prevent the child from suffering further distress by having to give evidence at a later stage, the provisions of sections 42/43 Children and Young Persons Act 1933 should be considered. This section provides that, if a doctor certifies that if a child were to give evidence it would seriously endanger the child's health, then a Magistrate may take a deposition from the child, which will be admissible as evidence, providing the accused or his legal representative had the opportunity to cross examine the child when the deposition was taken. A similar provision exists under section 103 Magistrates' Courts Act 1980 in relation to obtaining the evidence of children in committal proceedings for sexual offences. Appropriate cases should be drawn to the attention of the Crown Prosecution Service.

6.2 Expediting Proceedings

When prosecutions arise, committal proceedings and trials should be dealt with as sensitively and expeditiously as possible, in order to minimise further trauma to the child and reduce delays in preparation being made for the child's future.

7. GUARDIAN AD LITEM
7.1

Where a request is received from a Guardian ad Litem for copies of statements or documents obtained by police during an investigation of child abuse, and the case is likely to result in the prosecution of offenders, then the advice of the Crown Prosecution Service must be sought prior to disclosure. Where no prosecution is anticipated and the information is required for care or related proceedings, then with the consent of the witness *and* approval of the co-ordinator, or Metropolitan Police Solicitors where police have instituted care proceedings and are represented by them, such information including police statements and details of convictions, may be supplied. If witnesses ask for their particulars to remain confidential, then the contents of a statement may be disclosed so long as the identity of the witness is protected. (In the case of *D v NSPCC*, [1978] Appeal Cases page 171, it was held that the disclosure of an informant's details could be withheld in such instances.) Should details of the witness still be required, the witness should be interviewed, and the matter explained by the officer in charge of the child abuse team. If the witness still refuses to allow disclosure the matter is to be fully reported to Commander,

Community Involvement Policy Unit (TO30) who will decide whether the information should be revealed and the witness advised accordingly.

8. CASE CONFERENCES

8.1
Objectives

The object of a case conference is to assess and plan for the child's future and is therefore an essential feature of inter-agency co-operation. They are normally convened by social services departments, or the NSPCC but other agencies, including police, can request one if necessary. Where there is any conflict, the child's interests must transcend those of the parents. An initial conference may be quite large and will comprise of those people who can contribute materially to the proceedings, such as hospital and family doctors, police surgeons, health visitors, school teachers, social workers, etc. The conference will be chaired by a senior officer of the local social services department or the agency that convened it.

8.2
**Officers
to attend**

It is recommended that police officers who have actually undertaken the investigation should attend the case conference with their Detective Inspector. They will be in a better position than the case supervisor to answer any questions of fact, as well as being able to provide their own personal views on the investigation. Where emergency action has been taken by police, the officer(s) who took action could also be invited to attend the conference to describe what happened. In cases where there has been no police involvement prior to the case conference, an officer from the child abuse team should attend and if abuse is suspected that officer must inform the co-ordinator immediately.

8.3
**Disclosure
of information**

The success of joint investigation will pivot upon an open policy of full and frank exchange of information by all concerned. Officers have a wide discretion to disclose detail which can be used in the best interest of child victims. The disclosure of convictions of suspsects and other relevant intelligence held by police or social services can be conveyed to the other joint investigator as well as the case conference. (Home Office Circular 45/1986 Annex A, Para 2). However, when convictions are to be disclosed they should be submitted on Form 609 to the chairperson (ideally before the conference) who will be responsible for deciding which convictions are relevant and informing the conference of those details.

8.4
Supply of confidential information

The philosophy of a case conference is for the professionals present to contribute to the well-being of the child. This may mean divulging confidential information, including the reporting and assessment of rumours or gossip and breaching of confidences. Any dilemma as to the prudence of so doing should be judged against the possible effects upon child victims of withholding that information.

8.5
Decisions of case conferences

The chair of a case conference will endeavour to seek the joint agreement of those participating as to the proposed action, whether it be to prosecute the offender, institute care or wardship proceedings, inclusion of the child on the Child Protection Register, or arrange for voluntary supervision. Certain recommendations such as the termination of access by the parents or the assumption of parental rights, require the approval of the local Social Services Committee. In arriving at a decision due regard must be given by police and social services departments to each other's specific responsibilities and lines of accountability through the Home Secretary and Social Services Committees respectively. On this understanding, whilst the policy of the Metropolitan Police is one of commitment to a joint approach in the protection of children and the rehabilitation of their families, officers may still finally have to address

Unilateral action

the question of taking unilateral action, by way of further investigation and/or prosecution, contrary to the recommendations of the case conference. This is because it is the fundamental Common Law duty of police to keep the peace, included in which is the duty to detect crime and bring offenders to justice. There will be occasions when the detrimental effect of an individual child of being interviewed and called to give evidence in court will be outweighed by the greater public interest of protecting society from the perpetration of crime. (See also para 4.6)

8.6
Commander's Authority

Where such dissent occurs, further action should be suspended until a decision has been made by the chief officer of police, who in Metropolitan cases will be the Area Commander (Operations). Clearly such decisions could create a potential conflict and should be resorted to only in exceptional circumstances. Commanders must satisfy themselves that any decision reached is made in the best interests of the child victim and society, having first consulted the Director of Social Services, who should also be informed promptly of the final police decision and the action to be taken.

8.7
Claims for
Compensation

When a child has suffered personal injury, either physically or mentally, consideration should be given to obtaining compensation. If the child is in care then a claim to the Criminal Injuries Compensation Board may be made on the child's behalf by the Director of the relevant social services department. Whenever a key worker is appointed to a case of child abuse where the victum is taken into care, he/she should be reminded of the CICB scheme and asked to recommend the making of a claim through the local Director of Social Services. When the child is not taken into care, the responsibility for ensuring that applications are made for the compensation for victims of physical and sexual abuse rests with police who may need to rely on other agencies to bring suitable cases to attention. On receipt of a claim the Criminal Injuries Compensation Board will then ask the police for a report of the incident. It is important therefore that in the interests of the child, all allegations of abuse should be reported to police at the earliest opportunity. The Board will entertain claims submitted up to three years from when the incident occurred but compensation will not be paid unless the Board is satisfied that the offender will not benefit from any award. In granting an award the Board will appoint trustees to hold the compensation for the benefit of the child, making such provisions for maintenance and education as necessary. Trustees will be appointed even where the child remains in the family home. Compensation for the victims of child abuse, whose lives have been blighted, is essential.

8.8
Minutes of
conference

All professionals attending a case conference should retain a record of the items discussed and decisions reached. Full minutes will be taken and these are usually distributed to all those attending. These should contain a clear statement as to the confidentiality of material contained therein. If for any reason those invited are unable to attend the conference, they should submit their contribution in writing to the chairperson. They should expect to receive copies of the minutes and act upon the decision made. The mere fact that minutes will be provided does not obviate the necessity for police to take notes for the purposes of the investigation, and they should do so especially where it is a local practice to provide only a summary record of the meeting in lieu of full minutes. In such cases police may nevertheless request (and pay for) a full set of minutes where this is felt to be necessary. 'Summary Minutes' must NOT be accepted as being correct unless the officers concerned have seen and checked a copy of the full case conference minutes.

8.9
Review
Conferences

When the case conference decides to review the case at a later date to assess the progress made, the police co-ordinator should encourage the participation of police, unless circumstances make this unnecessary or impracticable.

8.10
Parents
attending Case
Conferences

In conjuction with the DHSS policy the Metropolitan Police considers it may *not* be appropriate for parents to attend formal inter-agency case conferences, consequently this issue must be fully discussed during the negotiation process within which joint investigations are established. In instances where agreement cannot be reached, police must endeavour to pursue their responsibilities keeping the best interests of the child in mind. Where parents do attend and difficulties arise, details will be reported to the Area Detective Chief Superintendent who will liaise with the Director of Social Services and explain the implications of parents attending case conferences in these circumstances. Should the Director decline to change the policy on this matter, the full facts are to be reported to the Commander Community Involvement Policy Unit (TO.30) who will advise as to future action in such cases. In other cases joint investigation will, it is believed, remove the possibility of embarrassment to police and social services through feeling inhibited in disclosing confidential details to which the conference may be entitled. In instances where parents are not suspected, police must keep them fully informed of the progress of the investigation.

9. CHILD PROTECTION REGISTER
9.1

Whenever a decision is made to include on, or to remove a child from the Register, the police officer from the child abuse team attending the conference will cause local and central records to be immediately made up or cancelled, giving full details of the conference decisions. It is essential that central records are accurately maintained, especially in respect of the Child Protection Register. This can only be achieved by prompt notification to Juvenile Index (SO5 Branch) by telephone as soon as changes in the child's circumstances are brought to the attention of police, and in submitting forms 87,88 and a copy of the relevant crime report where appropriate for registration as a GN88 (Non-accidental injury to children) docket immediately after the initial case conference. Details must be promptly attached to the docket on its return either from SO5, or from General Registry. These details must be in the form of either copies of the conference minutes with a covering report on form 728, or in the absence of conference minutes for reasons beyond the control of police a brief resume should be given on form 728, with the decisions clearly shown. It should be noted that because of the confidential nature of case conference notes, they must only be attached to GN 88 dockets and *not* CR files. All other occasions on which police have dealings with juveniles, ie other than at case conferences, must be fully reported on form 78 and submitted to SO5 Juvenile Index, through the relevant child abuse team. Provision should be made for regular reviews of the information held by those monitoring the development of the child, and the relationship of the family. Police should ensure that the sharing of information to maintain these records is for the benefit of those children whom they include, they must therefore be accurate and up-to-date.

9.2
General
Registry

General Registry holds all case files of abused children. It is essential that officers check with General Registry to ascertain if there is already a file opened on the family in question. If it transpires that there is one, it can only be drawn on the authority of the co-ordinator of the child abuse team, It is the responsibility of the child abuse team to ensure that the file is then fully updated and submitted to SO5 to enable them to revise their records. It is also imperative that Juvenile Index (SO5) be contacted by phone at this stage. This is (a) to ascertain if there is any further information which could be of assistance to the case conference, as well as to the investigation, and (b) so that SO5 are kept fully updated as to the current status of the case.

9.3
Infant
Deaths

Detective Chief Superintendents are to make local arrangements to ensure that Coroners are informed immediately by hospital authorities of all deaths involving infants (under 2 years of age) that are of a suspicious or unnatural nature, including cot deaths. On receipt of such a report, Coroners' Officers are to inform the Detective Chief Superintendent or his/her deputy without delay.

10. AREA REVIEW COMMITTEES
10.1
Detective Chief
Superintendent
to attend

It is essential for Detective Chief Superintendents, or in *exceptional circumstances*, their nominated deputy, a Detective Superintendent, to attend Area Review Committees in order that Force policy may be presented. Police co-ordinators and Detective Inspectors in charge of child abuse teams may be nominated to attend sub-committe meetings where policy matters are not at issue. To complement the police representation on Area Review Committees consideration should be given to the regular attendance of the Area Community Liaison Officer.

11. CASE PAPERS
11.1
Case Papers

The child abuse co-ordinator will be responsible for certifying that case papers have been properly completed and recommend them being 'put away' in General Registry after being noted in SO5, or marked for review in cases where children are still included on the Child Protection Register. All such recommendations must be forwarded through the Area Detective Chief Superintendent who will minute the papers accordingly.

12. PREVENTION
12.1

The prevention of child abuse requires the co-operation of the community. In recognition of this premiss the Metropolitan Police will endorse and where appropriate, provide tangible assistance for any programme which offers support to families at risk.

12.2
Publicity

This Force has a major role to play in the current situation of increased public awareness of abuse by developing expertise in working for children. The Force will publicise its work in this field to all officers, the agencies involved, as well as the general public.

12.3
Crime Prevention programmes

With the emphasis on prevention, current direct contact initiatives will be maintained and enhanced to include child abuse. The Force will seek the evolution of co-ordinated prevention programmes with Area Review Committees and central authorities.

APPENDIX 'A'

Extract from
HOME OFFICE CONSOLIDATED CIRCULAR
TO THE POLICE ON CRIME
AND KINDRED MATTERS

APPENDIX 3 — PARAS. 16–18

HOME OFFICE CIRCULAR NO. 179/1976

INVESTIGATION AND PROSECUTION

16. *In this context, as in all others, the prosecution of offences is a matter which rests by law within the discretion of the chief officer of police concerned, who may in some serious cases need to consult the Director of Public Prosecutions. In considering the exercise of their discretion in a particular case chief officers of police will no doubt take into account so far as possible any views expressed by case conferences on the question of prosecution.*

17. *In considering the need for an investigation, the Departments hope that where a case conference has been held chief officers of police (whilst retaining the capacity to take independent action) will take into account any views expressed by the conference about the effect of an investigation on the welfare of the child. Generally, where an investigation arises from the disclosure of information at a case conference, the person by whom the information is given should be informed that an investigation is to be made.*

18. *Where the police representative attending a case conference dissents from the view of other participants and thinks it right to take action (for example by way of investigation or prosecution) contrary to what they recommend, he should suspend further action until a decision has been made by the chief officer of police. Where the chief officer of police decides to take action contrary to the recommendations of a case conference, he should notify the other members of the proposed action and the reasons for it in line with the advice issued by DHSS to health and local authorities in February 1976. Where possible this notification should be given before the action is taken.*

Recommendations of the Cleveland Report

Recommendations
1. Recognition of Sexual Abuse
There is a need :
    a. To recognise and describe the extent of the problem of child sexual abuse;
    b. To receive more accurate data of the abuse which is identified.

2. Children
There is a danger that in looking to the welfare of the children believed to be the victims of sexual abuse the children themselves may be overlooked. The child is a person and not an object of concern.

We recommend that :
    a. Professionals recognise the need for adults to explain to children what is going on. Children are entitled to a proper explanation appropriate to their age, to be told why they are being taken away from home and given some idea of what is going to happen to them.
    b. Professionals should not make promises which cannot be kept to a child, and in the light of possible court proceedings should not promise a child that what is said in confidence can be kept in confidence.
    c. Professionals should always listen carefully to what the child has to say and take seriously what is said.
    d. Throughout the proceedings the views and the wishes of the child, particularly as to what should happen to him/her, should be taken into consideration by the professionals involved with their problems.
    e. The views and the wishes of the child should be placed before whichever court deals with the case. We do not however, suggest that those wishes should predominate.
    f. Children should not be subjected to repeated medical examinations solely for evidential purposes. Where appropriate, according to age and understanding, the consent of the child

should be obtained before any medical examination or photography.

g. Children should not be subjected to repeated interviews nor to the probing and confrontational type of 'disclosure' interview for the same purpose, for it in itself can be damaging and harmful to them. The consent of the child should where possible be obtained before the interviews are recorded on video.

h. The child should be medically examined and interviewed in a suitable and sensitive environment, where there are suitably trained staff available.

i. When a child is moved from home or between hospital and foster home it is important that those responsible for the day to day care of the child not only understand the child's legal status but also have sufficient information to look after the child properly.

j. Those involved in investigation of child sexual abuse should make a conscious effort to ensure that they act throughout in the best interests of the child.

3. Parents

We recommend:

a. The parents should be given the same courtesy as the family of any other referred child. This applies to all aspects of the investigation into the suspicion of child sexual abuse, and should be recognised by all professionals concerned with the family.

b. Parents should be informed and where appropriate consulted at each stage of the investigation by the professional dealing with the child, whether medical, police or social worker. Parents are entitled to know what is going on, and to be helped to understand the steps that are being taken.

c. We discuss below the position of parents in case conferences.

d. Social Services should confirm all important decisions to parents in writing. Parents may not understand the implications of decisions made and they should have the opportunity to give the written decision to their lawyers.

e. Parents should always be advised of their rights of appeal or complaint in relation to any decisions made about them or their children.

f. Social Services should always seek to provide support to the family during the investigation. Parents should not be left isolated and bewildered at this difficult time.

g. The service of the place of safety order on parents should include a written explanation of the meaning of the order, the position of the parents, their continuing responsibilities and rights and advice to seek legal advice.

4. Social Services

We make the following recommendations with regard to Social Services:

a. Place of safety orders should only be sought for the minimum time necessary to ensure protection of the child.

b. Records related to the use of statutory powers on an emergency basis should be kept and monitored regularly by Social Services Departments.

c. A code of practice for the administration by social workers of emergency orders for the purposes of child protection including the provision of information to parents defining their rights in clear simple language should be drawn up (see also recommendations on the courts).

Access

d. Whenever and however children are received into care social workers should agree with parents the arrangements for access unless there are exceptional reasons related to the child's interests not to do so. In either event the parent should be notified in writing as soon as possible of the access arrangements and the avenues of complaint or appeal open to them if they are aggrieved.

Case Conferences

e. Parents should be informed of case conferences and invited to attend for all or part of the conference unless, in the view of the Chairman of the conference, their presence will preclude a full and proper consideration of the child's interests.

f. Irrespective of whether parents attend the conferences, social workers have a primary responsibility to ensure that the case conference has information relating to the family background and the parents' views on the issues under consideration.

g. In complex cases the Chairman of the conference must be able to call upon the attendance of a qualified lawyer to assist in the evaluation of evidence indicative of care proceedings.

h. When a case conference is presented with medical opinions that are in conflict the doctors involved should be asked to review their findings jointly with the interests of the child in mind. If they are unable to establish common ground then they should be asked to identify the basis of their differences. It would then be for the case conference to consider their views in the context of the other information available.

Management

i. Senior managers in Social Services Departments need to ensure that they have efficient systems available to allow accurate monitoring of service activity which will alert them to problems that need to be resolved.

j. Staff engaged in social work practice in the field of child abuse and child sexual abuse need structured arrangements for their professional supervision and personal support. The work is stressful and it is important that their personal needs are not overlooked.

k. We recommend that careful consideration be given to the provision of structured systems of support and supervision for staff undertaking work on Emergency Duty Teams.

Operationally such teams should report to a senior line
manager.

l. Social Services Departments should maintain an open continuing relationship with the Police to review areas of mutual
concern.

5. Police

We make the following recommendations with regard to Police
Forces :

a. The Police should examine their organisation to ensure there
is an adequate communication network to achieve the recognition and identification of problems at operational level and
a system to develop remedies.

b. The Police should develop, monitor and maintain communication and consultation with the other agencies concerned
with child protection.

c. The Police should develop and practise inter-agency working, including joint planning and interviews of children in
investigation of sexual abuse within the family or caring
agency.

d. The Police should recognise and develop their responsibility
for the protection of the child as extending beyond the collection of evidence for court proceedings. This should
include their attendance at case conferences and assistance
to the other child protection agencies.

6. The Medical Profession

We make the following recommendations with regard to the
medical profession :

a. They should agree a consistent vocabulary to describe physical signs which may be associated with child sexual abuse.

b. There should be investigation of the natural history and the
significance of signs and symptoms which may be associated
with child sexual abuse.

c. Consideration be given to inquiring into the significance of
the phenomenon of anal dilatation.

d. Doctors engaged in the care of a child in whom the suspicion of sexual abuse is raised must of course give the child the appropriate medical care, but should also recognise the importance of the forensic element.

The doctor concerned should recognise the importance:

i. of taking a full medical history and making a thorough medical examination.

ii. of making where appropriate investigations for forensic purposes, for sexually transmitted diseases and for pregnancy in older girls.

iii. of completing full and accurate medical records which should provide the information for the protective agencies and on occasions the courts. [see appendix F] Those records should be made at the time of examination.

iv. of preparing statements for police purposes and/or for Social Services or NSPCC.

We understand that the Standing Medical Advisory Committee to the DHSS are in the course of providing guidelines for the medical profession on this subject.

e. On a medical examination for forensic or other evidential purposes unconnected with the immediate care and treatment of the child the informed consent of the parents should be sought. This may present difficulties for the police surgeon or doctor from the approved panel on the specialist assessment team [see below] in cases of suspected sexual abuse within the family. This problem needs to be considered further.

f. Medical practitioners who have examined a child for suspected sexual abuse and disagree in their findings and conclusions should discuss their reports and resolve their differences where possible; in the absence of agreement identify the areas of dispute, recognising their purpose is to act in the best interests of the child.

7. Area Review Committees/Joint Child Abuse Committees

We make the following recommendations in respect of the Area Review Committees/Joint Child Abuse Committees:

a. They should review the arrangements for identifying and monitoring suitable training for professionals working with child sexual abuse;

b. The membership of these committees should include those who have the authority and responsibility to bind their agency to implementing the recommendations of the Committee, and to play a useful part in the decision-making process which accurately reflects the view of the agency they represent.

8. Inter-Agency Co-operation

We strongly recommend:

a. The development of inter-agency co-operation which acknowledges:

i. no single agency—Health, Social Services, Police or voluntary organisation has the pre-eminent responsibility in the assessment of child abuse generally and child sexual abuse specifically. Each agency has a prime responsibility for a particular aspect of the problem. Neither children's nor parents' needs and rights can be adequately met or protected unless agencies agree a framework for their inter-action. The statutory duties of Social Service Departments must be recognised;

ii. careful consideration must be given to the detail of working arrangements between doctors, nurses, social workers, police, teachers, staff of voluntary organisations and others responsible for the care of children;

iii. arrangements for collaboration between services must not inhibit prompt action by any professional or agency where this is demanded by the best interests of the child. Agreements over collaborative work should not inhibit or preclude doctors, social workers or policemen from carrying out their primary professional responsibilities. The responsibility for the decisions will remain theirs;

iv. practical issues need to be recognised and resolved at local level in careful discussion between the respective agencies. For example:

• what the level of suspicion of physical or sexual abuse should be before the Police are informed that an offence appears to have been committed;

• when and what parents are told when doctors see signs that may be indicative of sexual abuse;

• in what circumstances social workers should delay seeing parents until they have been interviewed by the Police.

v. managers should accept responsibility for ensuring that agreements reached are implemented in practice. Each agency should give an undertaking not to make unilateral changes in practice or policy without giving prior notice to the others;

vi. the existence of bodies charged with the responsibility to co-ordinate practice between agencies does not relieve Chief Officers such as the Director of Social Services, the Chief Constable, the Director of Education and the Health Service District General Manager of their responsibility to ensure effective co-operation and collaboration between their services or to identify problems and seek solutions.

b. The establishment of Assessment Teams.

i. The function of the Specialist Assessment Teams (SAT) is to undertake the full multi-disciplinary assessment of the child and the family in cases of particular difficulty. Each member of the team will have direct access to information available within their agency. The completion of a medical examination, a social work assessment, and appropriate inquiries by the Police, carried out in a planned and co-ordinated way should allow the Specialist Assessment Team to present their joint assessment and conclusions to the referring agency or a case conference. Whilst each member of the team has a duty to act with care and undertake the full range of responsibilities normally ascribed to the individual's role—their primary responsibility as a team is to make an assessment. The duty to provide on-going treatment or plan for the future should remain with others.

ii. The team should consist of an approved medical practitioner, a senior social worker, and a police officer with sufficient authority to co-ordinate the investigation of cases.

iii. In each area a list of approved doctors should be drawn up. The process of approval might be adapted from the regulations under the Mental Health Act which provide for the approval of doctors for the purpose of that Act. The doctors on the list should have knowledge and experience of the needs of children and an understanding of child abuse in general and child sexual abuse in particular. They should be prepared, at the request of their medical colleagues, Social Services or the Police, to examine a child and participate in a formal multi-disciplinary assessment of the child's presenting concern. This may include collecting forensic evidence; compiling medical evidence for care proceedings; and involve attendance at case conferences and at Court. The doctors included on such a list might be community or hospital paediatricians, or those who have appropriate experience such as women police doctors, police surgeons etc.

iv. The Social Services will need to appoint to an approved list those social workers who are trained, experienced and competent in work in the field of child abuse and child sexual abuse.

v. The Police will need to appoint to an approved list, police officers trained, experienced and competent in the field of child sexual abuse to undertake the work required.

vi. It is probably not in the interests of either the children, families or professionals or the agency for staff—doctors, social workers, or police, to specialise solely in child sexual abuse. A special interest reflected in allocated time, complemented with other less-demanding work is the most likely arrangement to avoid stress and ensure a balanced perspective.

vii. The existence of the team will have the advantage of building a reservoir of expertise in a difficult area of work. The intention is to foster teamwork and co-ordination of activity without undermining primary professional responsibility or agency function. Such an arrangement would facilitate the development of skills amongst a wider group of people whilst ensuring a reservoir of specialist skills that staff could turn to for assistance with the difficult cases. It should have access to specialist expertise—for example a child psychiatrist or gynaecologist, who would be consulted or brought in on cases of particular difficulty.

c. The following framework and methods of working.

i. The flowchart gives a general outline. It does not cover every possibility. The framework is intended to allow straightforward cases to be dealt with in a straightforward way. It is not suggested that the Specialist Assessment Team deal with all referrals.

ii. All agencies—Police, Social Services, NSPCC, Health, will receive some referrals where there is a clear account of events by a child and/or an admission of guilt by a perpetrator.

• Social Services will receive information or referrals which present a straightforward pattern of information, clear account by a child, admission by a perpetrator and confirmation by a medical examination. Such cases will require Social Services to work closely with the Police and medical colleagues in a planned intervention. Evidence and information will be collated. A case conference will be called to ensure that all relevant information has been gathered and the conference recommendations are considered in the making of the final decisions in relation to civil or criminal proceedings.

• Referrals to doctors are most likely to arise in relation to an injury or disorder. Where an allegation by a child accompanied by primary medical signs allows a definitive conclusion to be drawn, the case will need to be referred directly to the Police and/or Social Services. In cases where suspicion is raised by the presence of physical signs without complaints by the child or a third party, a referral should be made to the Specialist Assessment Team for assessment.

• A number of such cases will involve allegations of offences made to the Police by a child or third party relating to events which have taken place outside the family. Such cases will normally be investigated and prosecuted by the Police without the involvement of other agencies. It may be necessary for the Police to draw on the skills of a doctor from the approved list to undertake a medical examination for evidential purposes. If during the course of their investigation, the Police become concerned about the adequacy of care and control the child involved is receiving in his/her own home, then referral to Social Services will need to be considered. Similarly, if the offences alleged to have been committed are such as to raise questions about the safety and welfare of any children within the household to which the alleged perpetrator belongs, referral of that consideration to the Social Services Department may be appropriate.

iii. All agencies, Police, Social Services, NSPCC, and Health, should refer cases to the Inter-Agency Team when they are presented with or become suspicious of the possibility of sexual abuse having occurred on the basis of physical or behavioural signs alone or where there is uncertainty as to whether or not abuse has occurred.

iv. When child sexual abuse within the family comes to the attention of the Police they should inform Social Services and consider the advisability of using the Specialist Assessment Team.

There may be other cases of complexity where the use of the Specialist Assessment Team is appropriate.

vi. If there is a suspicion of child sexual abuse in the mind of the professional, the danger of false identification ought

A framework for inter-agency response

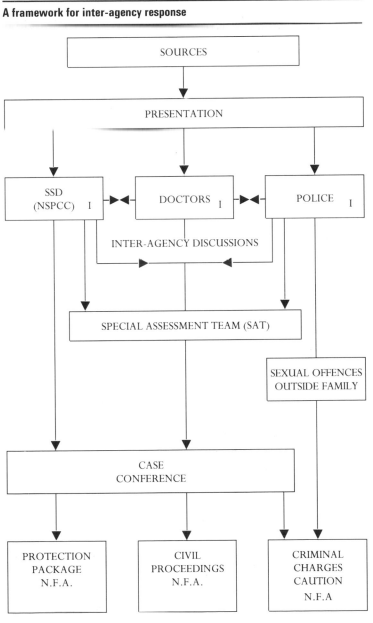

I = INFORMAL INQUIRIES   N.F.A. = NO FURTHER ACTON

not to be forgotten. Therefore when a suspicion arises the professional may elect to:

- take no further action;
- hold a watching brief;
- make further informal inquiries ([I] on the flowchart).

The level of concern may reach a point within the guidance agreed with other agencies—see a.iv above—where it is the duty of all professionals to inform others or refer to the Specialist Assessment Team.

    vii. The Specialist Assessment Team would normally be expected to present their findings to a case conference who will consider that information in the overall context of the case and make recommendations as to further action. Whilst professional suspicion may be justified in a particular case, recommendations by a case conference to pursue a statutory intervention under child care law must be firmly based on evidence that can be elicited and brought before a Court. Where such evidence cannot be found but suspicion remains arrangements must be made for the continuing assessment of the child.

9. Training

Training is one of the major needs shown by the Cleveland experience. We recognise that training requirements are different for each profession. We strongly recommend:

    a. Those responsible for the educational programmes of all disciplines involved in the care of children immediately consider the introduction of some instruction on the subject of child sexual abuse in basic training at student level.

    b. There should be general continuing in-service training for practitioners concerned with child care.

    c. There is an urgent need to give immediate in-service training to professionals to bring them up to date on child sexual abuse.

    d. The investigation and the management of the child and the family where there is suspicion of sexual abuse needs considerable professional skill. We recommend specialised training for experienced professionals with immediate responsibility for the children and their families.

From the evidence presented to the Inquiry there were particular issues which arose and needed to be addressed.

1. There is a need for inter-agency training and recognition of the role of other disciplines. For example police officers and social workers designated to interview children should have joint training in their approach to this task.

2. Police training needs to be developed well beyond the acquisition of knowledge in respect of the criminal offences involved.

3. The medical profession needs to appreciate the legal implications of and their responsibility for the evidential requirements of their work.

4. Those who work in this field must have an empathy with children and 'their feet on the ground'. They must be able to cope with the stress that is experienced by all who deal with these children. It should not be seen as a failure for some to take the sensible course of saying that he/she is not suited to do that sort of work.

5. In a rapidly changing and difficult area there is a need to review and evaluate the effectiveness of the programmes arranged.

6. All lawyers engaged in this type of work including Judges and Magistrates should have a greater awareness of and inform themselves about the nature of child abuse and the management of children subjected to abuse and in particular sexual abuse.

10. Courts

We make the following recommendations with regard to court proceedings:

a. Place of Safety Orders

i. There should be a statutory duty upon the Clerk to the Justices to keep records of all place of safety orders.

ii. Applications for place of safety orders should normally be made in the first instance to the Juvenile Court during court hours, and only if the court is not sitting or the application cannot be heard within a reasonable time to a single Magistrate.

iii. A simple written explanation of the meaning and effect of a place of safety order should be provided to parents or others served with such an order. This explanation would also be useful for all those who may have the responsibility to care for a child who is the subject of the order (for example foster parents or nursing officers).

b. Termination of access on an interim care order

The use of the provisions of section 12B for termination of access and the interpretation of the decision in R v. Bolton Metropolitan Borough Council ex parte B [1985] FLR 343 highlight existing difficulties over access and add urgency to the need to implement the proposals in the White Paper.

c. Consideration should be given to the practice in the Juvenile Courts of attendance of children in court in highly charged cases with members of the press and large numbers of people present. We would urge Magistrates to dispense with the attendance of the child or to arrange to see the child in a private room. It is an appropriate situation to seek the views of the older child as to attendance at court.

The Law on Child Care and Family Services Cm62

We strongly endorse the proposals set out in the White Paper and believe that it is now urgent that they should be implemented. We have considered that paragraphs 45 to 47, and paragraphs 54 to 68 were relevant to the Inquiry (See appendix J). We make the following recommendations on those paragraphs.

Emergency Protection Orders (paras 45 to 47)

a. A single Magistrate or the court should decide access if a Local Authority sees need to suspend it after an order has been granted on presumption of reasonable access.

b. Extension for 7 days should be in discretion of Magistrates and not restricted to 'exceptional circumstances'.

c. Application for the disclosure of the whereabouts of a child should include the power to commit to prison for refusal to comply.

d. Any dispute over medical examination during an extension of an emergency protection order should be decided by the court.

e. A simple explanatory pamphlet should be published setting out clearly the rights and duties of 'a person with actual custody'.

Juvenile Court

a. Extension of interim care orders should be at the discretion of Magistrates and not limited to 'exceptional circumstances.'

b. A dispute over access on the granting of and during the continuance of an interim care order should be decided by the Magistrates in the Courts.

c. On the granting of a custody order in care proceedings a Local Authority should have the right to make an allowance to the custodian, as in custodianship proceedings.

d. After care proceedings are instituted the Magistrates should have the power to determine, where necessary, interlocutory matters, such as further medical examinations of children for evidential purposes.

Wardship

a. Wardship should continue to play a role in care proceedings.

b. Parents should have the right to initiate wardship proceedings, subject to paragraph c below.

c. The President should regulate by Practice Direction the type of cases more fitted to be tried in the High Court.

Family Court

We recognise the considerable procedural advantages of the ability to move cases at any time from one tier of the Court to another, which would be achieved by the setting up of a Family Court.

Guardians ad litem

We are concerned that the independence of the guardian ad litem panel should be demonstrated and, in the absence of other arrangements for the administration of the panel, we commend the arrangement made between Cleveland Social Services Department and the Children's Society.

We further recommend:

a. 'Courts should appoint the guardians ad litem. A sufficiently large list of names should be submitted to enable a genuine choice to be made.'

b. An amendment to rule 14A 6(b) Magistrates Court (Children and Young Persons) Rules 1970 to define more closely the role of the guardian.

c. The Official Solicitor should first be invited to act for the child in wardship proceedings before any other guardian is appointed.

Media, Press and Public

We recommend that there should be rationalisation and clarity in:

a. The right of the press to attend court in the absence of the public. To protect anonymity of the child concerned, the decision whether any particular proceedings or part of proceedings is to be heard in public should be a decision for the tribunal hearing the proceedings in accordance with the usual procedure adopted in the High Court.

b. The right of the press and media generally to report on and publish information about children the subject of civil proceedings.

c. We strongly recommend automatic protection in all civil child proceedings, whether Juvenile or Domestic jurisdiction of Magistrates Court, County Court, or High Court including, matrimonial, guardianship and wardship; such protection should include a ban on publication of names, addresses, photographs or other identification of any child the subject of such proceedings. [see draft injunction in appendix K]

d. We recommend wider recognition by the media that the freedom of the press carries responsibility and consideration as to whether in situations such as arose in Cleveland it is in the best interests of a child to be identified.

11. Issues for further consideration

We wish to raise the following matters for further thought and wider discussion, but not by way of specific recommendation.

1. With the emphasis we place on the need to avoid the necessity of removing a child from home, Social Services Departments should consider the appropriateness of using their powers under s.1 of the 1980 Act designed to prevent the reception of a child into care, to defray for a limited period additional costs incurred by the suspected abuser in leaving home on a temporary basis while initial assessment is completed.

2. Samantha's story [page 9] leads us to advise that there needs to be more sensitive handling of teenagers who have been sexually abused.

3. There is a need to recognise the problem of adults who disclose abuse they suffered as children and the lack of help generally available.

4. There is a need to recognise the problems of an abuser who may wish to confess to the abuse but is inhibited from so doing by fear of the consequences. Some consideration might be given in certain circumstances to the wider interests of the child and the family and whether different arrangements might be made in suitable cases for those abusers who admit their guilt, who co-operate with the arrangements for the child and who are prepared to submit themselves to a programme of control.

5. We suggest that consideration is given to creating a new Office of Child Protection for use in care proceedings in the Family

Court with the following responsibilities :
    a. To scrutinise the application of the Local Authority in care proceedings and ensure that it is well founded.
    b. To call for additional investigation or reports.
    c. To invite the Local Authority or the Police to reconsider the civil or criminal proceedings proposed.
    d. To act as administrator of the guardian ad litem panel.
    e. Further consideration should be given to whether the office holder should ;
        i. direct who should be parties to the care proceedings
        ii. direct in which tier of the court it should be heard and
        iii. have the power to take no further action.